HOW TO COPE

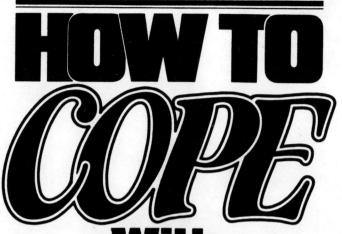

With conflict, crisis and change

Lloyd H. Ahlem

GL Regal Books

A Division of G/L Publications
Glendale, California, U.S.A.

Other good Regal reading
Do I Have to Be Me? by Lloyd H. Ahlem
Your Churning Place by Robert L. Wise
Caring Enough to Confront by David Augsburger
How to Be a Complete New You by Virginia Gold Apple

Scripture quotations in this publication are from the
New American Standard Bible. © The Lockman Foundation
1960, 1962, 1963, 1968, 1971. Used by permission.

Published by Regal Books Division, G/L Publications
Glendale, California 91209
Printed in U.S.A.

Library of Congress Catalog Card No. 77-94922
ISBN 0-8307-0581-3

contents

Everywhere I lecture, people ask the same question. "How can I cope?" In affluent sections of the United States and in remote regions of the world, the question is the same. The troubled woman at the PTA; the man who has been left with three preschool-age children by his wife's death; the 50-year-old executive, squeezed out of a high paying job by a merger of his company with a conglomerate; the African mother who has given birth to seven children, all of them born dead; a young man we met in Paris, escaping his family because he had adopted a religious faith contrary to his father's wishes; every victim of a crisis wants to know—what do I do now?

But crisis victims are not the only ones asking the question. So are those faced with great changes that are commonly thought of as promotions, improvements, and goals achieved. A wealthy manufacturer once told me, "I worked like a dog making my dough and thought that was tough. Now that I have it, what do I do? Spend it? Give it away? My life-style is so different I'm at a loss to adapt to all the comforts—and all the requests."

Or consider the parents I met during the first year I was working as a school psychologist. A handsome young four-year-old graced their home and perplexed them endlessly. He could read high school material and work fairly complicated mathematics problems. He rattled endless questions at them. When I tested him, his IQ was somewhere above 170; he insisted we quit the test to eat lunch so we never found out the final result. It probably wasn't important at that point anyway. He wrote a term paper for kindergarten social studies describing the geological structure of a volcano that erupted in a Mexican corn field a number of years ago and created a mountain on the spot. After hearing the paper, I was certain the exact IQ number wasn't important. But how do you live with a youngster like this? That's what mom and dad wanted to know. How do you cope?

All the great experiences of life involve the ability to cope. All the changes we experience test our adaptabilities. All the gifts with which we are endowed create expectations for their proper use. And with the rapid pace of living, moving, and changing, we are sometimes pressed to adapt more quickly and more frequently than we had planned. We are a multi-cultural people living in several different worlds. We have powers within us and expectations placed upon us that cause us to ask, "What do I do now?"

This book is an attempt to get a handle on how the mind works—how it copes. Most of us will never go to a psychiatrist or professional counselor. We will read some articles that flash a glimmer of light and we will share our mixed feelings with some close friends. Our wives or husbands or parents may offer some psychological support, but those will be the only resources outside ourselves we will bring to our life situations. So this volume is an attempt to gather some information from the fields of psychology, medicine and other disciplines that will help normal people get through the usual crises and changes of life, using their common human and spiritual endowments. It won't be the whole story by any means, but it just might help.

one

Life's Great Changes

Harold was an attorney specializing in labor relations for a large food processing and manufacturing firm. He traveled a good deal, but lived in the southwestern part of the United States. He spent several years getting settled into his new home and developing a pattern of life that he found comfortable and renewing to his spirit. To achieve this, he had to negotiate considerably with both his employer and his wife. His location was chosen after much discussion about his travel requirements and the kind of home his wife and family would like to have. Numerous compromises were worked out, most of them satisfactory to him and his family. With his company's cooperation he worked out his travel so that he would be home for substantial portions of time but away on business for substantial periods also. He agreed to take his vacations in the winter so that inconveniences to his company could be minimized. This meant that his children would not be with him at vacation time, and he would be working while school was out.

It seemed to Harold that his negotiations about living were about completed and most of the stressful questions had been resolved. Happy life was about to begin, and the realization of a number of dreams was imminent. In fact, during the first year under this arrangement, family affairs seemed to go better than at any time in the past. The home was expensive and lovely, the golf and tennis facilities near by. Schools were exempt from the problems of big city life. The church the family attended was pleasant and out of debt; it added just the right touch of value to their experiences. The employer's personal and social demands were within manageable limits so expectations were easily and pleasantly met. Not Utopia, but not bad!

Harold's company held its usual monthly management meeting just after he had returned from a brief but invigorating vacation. On this particular morning the atmosphere of the meeting was electric. The rumor mills were churning out reports of a major expansion of the business, and more than one junior executive had dreams of promotions flashing in his head.

The president called the meeting to order, grinning as he was seldom seen to do. "Gentlemen," he announced, "our firm is beginning one of the greatest ventures it has ever tackled. We are acquiring significant expansion facilities in the New York and Washington areas. These should provide a healthy challenge for many of you here today. This announcement will reach the papers shortly and the effects upon the value of your stock should be highly positive and significant."

Harold was struck with a case of galloping ambivalence. All previous company expansions had meant new opportunities for him and new additions to his personal wealth and income. He felt a real itch to see what he could do again in a similar venture. But he suddenly realized that for the past several years, he had been planning his life around his family and their nearly realized dreams. He had settled in, dug his wells, built his hut, and implied to his family that all the unsettlings of corporate life were pretty well past. Would he be rooted up and moved to another place? Or would the carefully negotiated arrangements and compromises be honored by his company in light of this new turn of events?

The company president continued his discourse. "This major move implies some interesting events in the lives of our corporate family members. A number of you will be asked to pull up stakes once again and meet the challenge this opportunity provides. Several of you will gain important promotions you have been dreaming about and hoping for. We will need the utmost cooperation from all of you and the company will do its best to make the changes well worth your while."

Harold began to feel a little sick. It just might be that he would be uprooted and shipped off to who knows what and where. But as the boss grinned, Harold felt himself grinning too and waiting for the next sentence. It came. "Our first request is that Harold, a long time employee with a significant record, become the general manager of the Washington operation. This may be difficult in light of his development of heaven here in the southwest, but a salary and benefits package worth about double his present remuneration will surely make all else pale into insignificance. Right, Harold?"

"Unbelievable," retorted Harold. He excused himself almost immediately to telephone his wife. But as he got to the phone, he sickened again. For the first time in their married lives he was genuinely afraid to share his so-called success. Instead of phoning he returned to the meeting to hear who else was getting the lift of his life. As several of the men heard their names, they shouted with glee; but not all. Some had worked out arrangements similar to Harold's, and he could tell they were less than ecstatic. Wonderings began. Would crisis and opportunity become the same thing in his life?

It was two weeks before Harold could break the news to his wife and family. During those two weeks he was sure he heard twice as many comments about how satisfied his family was with their present living arrangement. The house was more pleasant, the golf and tennis got better, the sermons on Sunday were more lifting, etc., etc. But sooner or later all had to know what was in the near future. When Harold broke the news at the dinner table one evening, there was stunned hush, then some tears, then his wife simply saying, "We know what business life is all about, don't we? And we'll make the best of it." All was silent after those words, except for some quiet sobbing by the two daughters who would reluctantly yield to the mother's comments.

Within a month the family had packed up, moved, sold their dream home and landed in suburban Washington. Harold was the new boss in a huge company and faced all the problems of an "imposter" manager. All personal relationships were new, both in business and at home. No family routine could be established since Harold was responsible for the whole operation and had to learn the business as well as supervise it. The hours were long though income was at an all time high. Harold didn't realize it, but all of the staff at the new company were going through their own crises as a result of the merger. And that led to more than one personal skirmish as the adjustments were being made.

In three months, Harold was unduly tired. His children were constantly badgered by their peers because they "talked southern." The family had failed to establish any new church relationship, and the wife was having a bad case of cabin fever in a plush suburban home.

Harold soon reached his saturation point with frustration, newness, change and general unhappiness. Without a word of family discussion, he phoned his company president and quit. He offered to stay on for 30 days while new management could be secured. But the president, who was incensed, ordered the locks changed on the office that very day. Harold went home that night leaping up the sidewalk, hugging his kids, astounding his wife. He began making plans for a whole new start in life. The crisis was over, but a new one might be just developing.

To conclude our story about Harold, he substantially altered his life-style, reduced his standard of living, and resettled his family in the western part of the country. This of course meant many readjustments, but in a year's time he was successfully engaged in a part-time law practice while his wife operated a gift shop in a small town. He had survived middle-aged occupational crisis, corporate fallout, and a reduced income. But his spirit was revived as he became active in a friendly church and learned to know a God who took a personal interest in the life of his family.

The year of transition from corporate mogul to country lawyer was no easy trip. He was plagued by guilt for having left his company so abruptly. Taking away a long list of luxuries from his family made him seem selfish. He felt he was putting them through a strain for his personal reasons. But he also felt exhilarated that he had the courage to make so bold a move. He felt good physically and mentally. His savings over the years sustained his shortages during this period. His investments proved valuable and he had a good deal of economic freedom. But he noticed he even felt a bit guilty about that. Few people in the world can cut loose from a substantial job and go free for a significant length of time. Why should he be so privileged? When his year of adjustment was over he described it as having gone through death and resurrection. He had cast himself entirely loose from his former life (a form of death); yet he was sustained through his crisis (and came to new life, or resurrection).

The death and resurrection theme seems to describe all kinds of normal changes in life. Even vacations that alter life significantly seem to have this character. The first few days away from home seem like a stunning mental episode. Then follows a period of depression, until the vacationer arrives back at work just in time to resurrect. Whenever we find ourselves in highly unfamiliar circumstances or under unusual conditions we experience a sense of loss—even when the conditions are those surrounding an event commonly regarded as positive.

A job promotion, a marriage reconciliation, a move to another geographic location—all these can be essentially positive events that trip off the crisis adaptations in us. I have discovered that when I have been traveling, seeing many interesting places and people, and speaking to stimulating audiences, and then return to my home and the more routine life, I experience in mild form the cycle of emotions that comes normally with crisis. A recent ten-day trip to Europe was such an occasion. Five days after we got home, my feelings "bottomed out" and I had to reenter normal life having experienced in pint-sized fashion the feelings one undergoes in a crisis.

Another example of the death and resurrection theme may be found in marriage. A wedding is one of the great happy events of life. The bride and groom are almost giddy with joy. They are so preoccupied with each other and because of their happiness they can hardly think straight—and sometimes that's the way they act. It is as though nothing in the world mattered but this great event. And for them that may be true.

A few months or a year may lapse before they speak objectively about their emotions. But if they are honest, they will often report that the cycle of death and resurrection was present in their emotions. They will inform you that the marriage with all its preparation formed a high moment—so high all else seemed insignificant. Then, beginning a few days or weeks later, their feelings began to die down. They began finding out the realities about each other. Bad breath, annoying habits, dull moments, and in-laws came to their attention. The facades so carefully constructed through romantic days wilted and real people walked out into full view. And it was downright depressing. But then the resurrection began and a normal life-style returned with new joys and new responsibilities.

The point of these illustrations is that in all of the great changes in our lives, whether in crisis or in death, or in great success and elation, the adaptive responses of people follow essentially the same pattern. Whether the impact event is the death of a spouse, a jail sentence for a family member, a giant promotion in business, or a happy marriage, the adaptive machinery of the human works about the same in all situations.

The romantic propaganda in American society has occasionally destroyed a potentially good marriage before it was well begun. I recall a young couple, both of them talented and of Christian conviction, who married in the midst of both spiritual and secular idealizations. Spiritual because they openly declared that their marriage was to be a testimony to the world of what the total Christian marriage could be. Secular because they courted in romantic terms, reenacting Hollywood's finest illusions of idealized love. But the honeymoon was scarcely over when the realities of actual people living together came crashing through their idealized imaginations. He thought sex was for both love and fun. She thought it was for procreation and to teach endurance of character. He tried to correct her behavior by quoting Bible verses. She thought his attitude was the result of a low quality of spiritual life.

The marriage did not survive this period, which may be called the *impact phase* of their problem. Had the couple known that such problems are common and understandable, they might have persevered to make a happy marriage. They believed the Hollywood phony baloney, but they did not know that there is a down side to every great change in life. Instead, they divorced a few months after their marriage and have spent ages trying to recover from a crisis that normally would have lasted no more than a year. The marriage died and they bailed out. Had they waited and sought reasonable counsel, resurrection could have taken place. Their feelings would have stabilized and they would have been much wiser and happier for it.

I have been told that the Chinese ideogram for crisis consists of two symbols—the figures that mean death plus opportunity. Perhaps the ancients had a handle on life changes that we are just now discovering and writing about. I hope that a discussion of the great changes of our lives might reduce the crisis dimensions and increase the opportunities for us, and that the peace that surpasses our comprehension may bless our lives in Christ (see Phil. 4:7).

two

Crisis in Change

In the first chapter we mentioned several of the great changes that come to us—death, promotion, marriage, loss of employment and others. Let's extend the list by noting a study that was done at the University of Washington. Dr. Thomas Holmes listed 43 crises and changes most likely to cause us problems of management, and established a rating scale that approximately measures the impact of these life-changing events. Dr. Holmes assigned a weight of 100 to the most serious of these events, gave other events lesser weights, and listed them in order of their degree of impact upon people. He further noted that if a person undergoes more than 200 impact units in any one 12-month period, he has experienced enough stress to warn him of danger. He has entered the high-risk category for possible physical or mental breakdown.

Dr. Ralph Hirschowitz, M.D., writing in the *Levinson Letter*, comments as follows concerning the research of Dr. Holmes.

> In studies conducted over the last 30 years, Dr. Holmes has found, as have others in the field, that serious illnesses are often preceded by a cluster of life events. Two hundred life-change units in a single year may be more than an individual can stand, and he may be headed for a major crackup. Widowers, for example, die 40 percent faster in the first six months than comparable peers . . . .
>
> Even if stress doesn't produce physical illness, it often exacts a mental and emotional price. At minimum, it weakens the reasoning powers, depletes physical energy, and creates an emotional imbalance that adversely affects his ability to work properly.[1]

Here is the list of life events noted by Dr. Holmes:[2]

Rank	Event	Impact Units
1	Death of a spouse	100
2	Divorce	73
3	Marital separation	65
4	Jail term	63
5	Death of close family member	63
6	Personal injury or illness	53
7*	Marriage	50
8	Fired from work	47
9*	Marital reconciliation	45
10	Retirement	45
11	Change in health of family member	44
12	Pregnancy	40

13	Sex difficulties	39
14	Gaining new family member	39
15	Business readjustment	39
16	Change in financial state	38
17	Death of close friend	37
18	Change to different line of work	36
19	Change in number of arguments with spouse	35
20	Mortgage over $10,000	31
21	Foreclosure of mortgage or loan	30
22	Change in responsibilities at work	29
23	Son or daughter leaving home	29
24	Trouble with in-laws	29
25*	Outstanding personal achievement	28
26	Wife begins or stops work	26
27	Beginning or end of school	26
28	Change in living conditions	25
29	Revision of personal habits	24
30	Trouble with employer, boss	23
31	Change in work hours or conditions	20
32	Change in residence	20
33	Change in schools	20
34	Change in recreation	19
35	Change in church activities	19
36	Change in social activities	18
37	Mortgage, loan less than $10,000	17
38	Change in sleeping habits	16
39	Change in number of family get-togethers	15
40	Change in eating habits	15
41*	Vacation	13
42*	Christmas	12
43	Minor violations of law	11

I have marked several of the items in the list with an asterisk. These are events usually thought of as highly positive events: marriage, reconciliation, outstanding personal achievement, vacation, and Christmas. The point is that even the positive stresses in life should be considered in any psychological cost-accounting of the changes we experience.

I had a colleague, a college teacher, who worked diligently at his scholarship for many years without much notice. Then he published an important finding that set the scientific world on its ear. Suddenly he was asked to appear at learned society conventions, make comments for the news media, and appear at business lunches. His achievement won a significant prize and international recognition. He was so overwhelmed with the attention and the accompanying stresses that he reeled at the impact. He hid himself in his office and arranged for all phone calls to be handled by the university switchboard. We hardly saw him for months. Furthermore, he was discouraged from further research for fear of the stress success might bring. He was a success casualty.

The understanding that success has its psychological cost has helped me to comprehend why some outstanding people have left important positions at the peak of their careers. They left, not because of difficulties or problems, but because they were successful and couldn't take it. You have heard the old saying about not being able to stand success; it's true at least in part.

Perhaps we should call this phenomenon "adulation accounting." It may explain why the sudden fame heaped upon a young rock star, actor, or professional athlete may be more than he or she can manage. It reminds me of a statement made by a philosophy teacher of mine: "Beware of what you desire most, you may get it!" Genuine grief, tension, irritability, even physiological disruption may accompany huge doses of success. Bouts of fatigue and mourning for loss of familiar achievements may appear.

But if the tensions are mastered, the successes will have a positive effect. If not, they can demolish a person and his career. One of my professors in graduate school concluded that those who achieve the most and survive it best are those who have a history of moderate successes throughout their lives, and have had to stretch psychologically to meet challenges without being overwhelmed by them. Furthermore, they have lived in an environment of positive regard from the most important people in their lives; parents, teachers and close friends.

So we must account for both the positive and negative experiences of our lives to measure the stresses that have been upon us. As you look at Dr. Holmes' list, you may be able to measure approximately your own burdens. Bear in mind that people vary a great deal in their capacity to withstand stress and that similar experiences vary greatly in their impact upon people. But it has been my observation that as I have discussed the list with various audiences, listeners often assess quite well how great or small are the stress factors in their lives.

Several years ago our family made a move from the west coast to the midwest; changing jobs, professions, geography, schools for the children, friends, neighbors, and some minor social customs. We certainly underestimated the impact such a move would bring. We survived it very well, but we have a new appreciation for the stresses caused by life changes, especially for business executives who are transferred frequently and for whom constant uprooting is a way of life. A little later on we shall discuss some steps people may take in managing such changes in life.

We are also discovering that changes in our society seem to have more impact and to come more frequently than in the past. A number of factors can be identified that may explain the increasing stress and tension we experience.

A Shifting Time Base

First, we find a shifting time base in our lives. This is much the story behind Alvin Toffler's book, *Future Shock*.[3] He notes that the time that elapses between a major technical discovery and the application of that discovery to a product in the marketplace has shortened markedly in the last generation or so. Where once it took many years between breakthrough and application, it is now only a matter of a few years. Thus we live with perpetual obsolescence of the goods we use. It seems to be of value to have some constancy of environmental objects in our lives. Dealing with the same objects and devices adds some stability, whereas with constant change we suffer some losses.

A second example of the shifting time base is apparent in our travel. Almost any one can move around the world in a matter of hours with little advance planning. Such was our experience recently when my son and I traveled to Africa to visit a mission field. The actual time spent traveling was about 22 hours, with time between flights for a bit of napping in a Paris airport. We went from Chicago to a Stone Age culture and back in a few days.

While in Africa we flew in a light plane with an African director of primary schools. It was the first time he had ever flown, and his reactions were most interesting. We took him from one village to another to visit schools he was supervising. Normally he spent an entire day trekking from one school to the other. But this time the entire flight took eight minutes. He looked at his watch frequently as we passed over familiar landmarks. He just shook his head as we landed. He found himself with a whole day for which he had no plans. We could tell the effect upon him was jolting. A new cultural wrinkle had been creased into his life.

Increased Power

A second major factor that changes the impact of events in our lives is the factor of increased power of people over each other. Every morning I drive a couple of tons of steel to work amidst fairly heavy traffic. If I chose, I could demolish both people and property as I travel. Likewise many others have considerable power over me. The fact is further illustrated by the possibilities of mass destruction through warfare. Many nations, both great and small, now possess the means to destroy much of the world. We are rapidly reaching a point where almost all of us hold a veto power over the existence of all others. The plain fact is that in the near future, nearly anyone can have complete power over anyone he may choose.

It is possible to anticipate a time when even a very small business or terrorist group can produce, unnoticed, mechanisms that would provide them with worldwide power. Small corporations could produce atomic weapons, for example. Or they could create biological substances capable of affecting millions of people. The great fact of our age is power and the resultant vulnerability it creates. It is no wonder our crises are amplified and our nerves more jumpy than in times past.

Rapid Change

Yet another factor in the increase of tensions is that of rapid change in social conventions and cultural norms. Changes in dress and changes in language occur so quickly that any sustained absence from a particular area can produce odd responses from those who recently have returned. Missionaries have told us that an absence from the United States for as little as two or three years creates all kinds of problems of appropriate dress and language when they return. In fact, one veteran missionary from South America confided that he hated to come home because reverse cultural shock at reentry to the U.S. was more difficult than the shock of going to South America for the first time. His difficulty was accented by his unrealistic expectations for an easy reentry. If he could, he would have preferred to take a vacation in the country to which he was assigned.

Widespread Exposure

On a recent trip to the Scandinavian countries I discovered yet another factor that amplifies our stress in life's changes. It is the factor of mass awareness of what is happening in the world. The time was, presumably, when much of the world's business could be conducted in quiet, secret places. Now, with the exposure of television and massive press organizations, everyone knows everyone else's business. The Swedes had ample and accurate information about the great political events in America. Newspapers and wire services in Copenhagen carried up-to-the-minute reports about the performance of the New York Stock Exchange. Almost any major corporate deal was instant news in western Europe. With so many people watching every action they take, it is no wonder that international business leaders are a bit jumpy.

A couple of years ago I assumed temporary duties as coach of the golf team at the college I serve as president. I didn't consider it a big deal—just seven fellows and a coach trying to win a few matches. But a big Chicago paper picked up the story and printed it in double column, seven inches long, on the sports page. The story also hit the wire services and people all over the country knew of my brief venture. An outstanding young golfer from central America applied for admission to my school. I experienced some stress because of the wide exposure of a part of my life.

More People Educated

We must also note that for the first time in the world's history we live in a culture where the masses have been educated to a level once reserved only for the elite. Depending upon the study you read, from 60 to 80 percent of the high school graduates in this country go on to further schooling. Furthermore, they have been exposed in public education to all the problems of the world, using the finest technical machinery ever assembled. We have huge numbers of people who are intellectually adequate to comprehend what is happening in the world. And when they comprehend, they want to participate. So we have dramatically increased the number of human transactions that must enter in to making any major public decision.

It was not so in the African countries we visited. We saw, instead, nations where less than a handful of people had been educated well enough to comprehend what was directly happening to them. And those who did comprehend were set at sea emotionally by the political machinations that were rolling over them. They were out of control of their own destinies and their resulting anxieties were great.

Some studies have indicated that job-related stresses have increased in recent years. The American Medical Association conducted a survey of 2,800 business executives in 1958. Thirty percent of the executives reported job-related personal problems: dissatisfaction with advancement possibilities; drinking at lunch; smok-

27

ing a great deal; excess worry over job decisions; job insecurity; problems of sleeplessness; achievements unrecognized; predinner cocktail in the evening.

The survey was repeated in 1973 and disclosed a marked increase in every symptom except smoking.

In another survey of 2,000 businessmen, 260 complained of excess tension on the job. In this study the stresses were highest in the 50-59 age bracket, among the self-employed, among lower management groups, and among women who were experiencing new equalities with men in executive roles. Respondents reported that 7 percent of the problems were physical in origin and 93 percent were the result of strain, tension and pressure. With regard to these studies the *Levinson Letter* states:

> This undoubtedly reflects a very costly loss to industry which ought to be minimized if at all possible.
>
> Contrary to the impression these surveys give, stress is in itself neither good nor bad: it's how a person reacts to it that makes the difference. If a person grows and masters a stressful situation, that's good; if he fails and his emotional and physical health deteriorate as a result, that's bad.
>
> However, people in business tend to think of stress as negative because the casualty rate is so high. And since change causes stress, and the pace of change is accelerating all the time, that trend is very likely to continue.[4]

Again, it is the point of this book to look at change and at our human ways of adapting, including the spiritual resources that will help us deal with change more healthfully.

Perhaps a specific definition of the term *crisis* will add

to our discussion. Dr. Ralph Hirschowitz, in a *Psychiatric Annals* reprint, defines crises as having several key characteristics:

A temporary condition. Personality systems are self adjusting, and therefore tend to self correct to some degree.

Mental, cognitive uncertainty. The uneasiness of not knowing what is happening or the outcome is a perceptible stress.

Psychophysiologic symptoms. The body reacts to the psychological stress. Aches, pains, eating problems, sleeplessness, general discomfort.

The situation has no exit. The demand for change is inescapable. Something must give. A terminal illness, a foreclosed mortgage, a deportation from a country, a consummated divorce, a lost job. The past cannot be repeated; change is a must.

Inadequate coping skills. One perceives approximately what must be done, but recognizes inadequacy to perform. He is in over his head.

Paralysis of thought or will. The stunning impact is such the victim cannot move on his own. Cannot plan action or seek help.

Exaggerated defense mechanisms. Too much rationalization, blaming others, compensating for losses, etc.

Experience of fear. Fear dominates life and accounts for whatever action or inaction is taken. Dependency. Behavior lacks balance and perspective.[5]

The person experiencing a significant number of the above characteristics has reached the impact phase of crisis. The problem has just landed on him and he has manifested his first responses. From this point on, many of his reactions depend upon his built-in capacities and the help he receives. The course of events can be approximately predicted and described, so we will turn our attention to these matters in the following chapters.

Notes

1. Thomas H. Holmes and Richard Rahe, Stress Rating Scale, *Journal of Psychosomatic Research*, 1967. Vol. 2, p. 216. Quoted from *The Levinson Letter* "Addendum."
2. Ralph G. Hirschowitz, "Addendum" a special feature of *The Levinson Letter* (Cambridge, Mass: The Levinson Institute, Inc., n.d.) p. 3.
3. Alvin Toffler, Future Shock (New York: Bantam Book, Inc., 1970), ch. 2.
4. "Addendum" p. 1.
5. Ralph G. Hirschowitz, "Crisis Theory: a Formulation," in *A Psychiatric Annals Reprint* (New York: Insight Publishing Co., Inc., n.d.).

three

Phase One:
The Impact Phase

At a recent summer conference I lectured on crisis, change, and the management of these experiences. Among the more casual of my listeners was a young married couple for whom life was going well and for whom much of this information was more academic than real. The couple's children were healthy and life-shaking crises were events that happened to other people. But not for long.

One week after the close of the conference, the young wife's father arose early from a night of fitful sleep and entered the bathroom. He had just opened the door when a stroke instantly ended his life—the angel of death had made a sudden visit.

This event obviously precipitated for his daughter all the social, religious, legal and economic aspects that are associated with death in our culture: notices to relatives, finding a will, caring for her mother, the legal aspects of access to the safe deposit box, completing business transactions necessary to the family enterprise.

In the midst of the crisis, the young wife had an appointment with her family doctor for a routine physical exam. This usually routine and simple event suddenly became a huge problem. The appointment was near the time of the funeral, and the abnormal fear that something might be wrong leaped into her consciousness. With the appointment changed, and the fears suppressed by major applications of will power, the young wife entered the physician's office. He soothed her considerably, but then discovered several cysts developing on her neck. Now she was shaking with anxiety again and had to submit to a biopsy.

The days between funeral and biopsy were sheer agony. The young woman had great difficulty sleeping, and lost her ability to organize her household. Her husband had to take a day or two off from work and pitch in. He was a little miffed since he had always perceived his wife as easygoing and above all minor irritations. In his mind a funeral was something that came into the lives of everyone, and a biopsy is routine, so why all the fuss?

The minor surgery was done in the doctor's office and lab tests ordered. In a few days the reports came. "Uncertain diagnosis, possible malignancy, excision recommended," stated the terse lab reply. The poor woman was shattered and her husband was angry; angry that a routine medical procedure should upset his household so badly. He clearly underestimated the full impact of the problem. But he bit his tongue, and cooperated with wife and doctor. The surgery was performed. It was successful, so only the problems of the father's departure remained.

Home again from the minor surgery and recovering both in body and spirit, the couple took time to reflect upon their feelings and behavior. Their relationship had been momentarily strained and they recognized they had a bit of patching up to do. Then it occurred to them that they had just been through a recent discussion of crisis and change. They thought what they had heard might now be of value. As they reviewed the subject they had no difficulty concluding that they were just past the "impact phase" of their problems.

At this point, let's identify the four phases of any great life-changing event or crisis. These are: Impact, Withdrawal-Confusion, Adjustment, and Reconstruction-Reconciliation. We shall deal with each of these in turn and then summarize with a chart at the end of the discussion of the four phases.

Impact Phase Is Short

The *impact phase* is usually quite short. It does not take a lot of time to perceive that you have been jolted by something of major proportions. Furthermore, it is only a short time until the adjustive mechanisms of the mind begin to do their work, sometimes automatically. Therefore the impact phase is that part of the problem when the crisis becomes known and the stunning effect is upon us. Usually the time period is from a few hours to a few days. For example, the death of a loved one will hit us hard and give us a few days of incapacitation and numbness. Often the tears of full realization come some hours after the event has occurred.

In some crises the time of the impact phase might be a little longer. For example, I know of divorce situations where it took a number of days to absorb the blow because one partner could not believe the action of the other. In such cases there had been no open fighting and the realities of the unhappiness were well hidden. But in most situations, the time elements are quite short in the impact phase of our problems.

In the impact phase of crisis or change, the person makes a most important decision. It is what psychologists call the *fight or flight decision.* It is the answer to the question, "Shall I stay and battle this thing through, or shall I duck and run, or ignore the whole thing?" The decision may be made somewhat unconsciously. Since we are usually less than fully competent at impact, our acquired tendencies in behavior may move us to choose one direction or the other. The person who has most often ignored realities of problems may be set up to try the flight method. On the other hand, if a person has attacked problems all his life, he will unconsciously set himself up to lick whatever besets him.

I have known people who have faced terminal illness by ignoring it, often shortening their lives by many years. One man refused to go to the doctor for fear of what he might learn. He was deathly afraid of cancer and did not want to face the possibility that he might have it. What he really had was a minor internal infection that eventually destroyed his kidneys. Had he obtained proper treatment he would have lived many more years. Instead we sadly laid him to rest in his early sixties.

On the other hand we have all known those who have overcome mountainous obstacles to make significant achievements. It is quite clear to mental health professionals that the "fight" response is by far the healthiest in a time of crisis. It is the response that keeps one from distorting realities and prompts him to mobilize the best resources he has, sometimes discovering aptitudes and endurance he did not know he possessed. I once worked with a young boy who was born with hydrocephalus, cerebral palsy, strabismus, and spina bifida, and without hip sockets. But he was determined to learn to walk and go to school just like all the other kids. He did walk, although with crutches. His pediatrician told me that his life was one huge headache. His hydrocephalus gave him a pain known only to habitual boozers after a long drinking bout. But this lad fought and prayed his way into outstanding achievement in school. One of his proudest moments was the time he fell out of a tree. He was overjoyed because he had succeeded in climbing the thing!

The "flight" response seems to prolong the crisis sequence. Each succeeding phase is dependent upon the adjustments made in the previous one. If you avoid reality you cannot make a proper adjustment, and so you prolong the painful aspects of a great change in life. Someone going through a tough time needs a friend who will stay close and keep him from fleeing the scene. This friend must, however, avoid crowding the victim too much, or a secondary problem may develop—a poor personal relationship between the two.

During the impact phase of any great change or crisis in our lives, our intellectual processes are not at their best. We are characterized by numbness and disorientation. Many people report that they could not think or feel during the hours of impact. Some studies have shown that under stress we tend to think simplistically, stereotypically, and without great insight. We will sometimes repeat unsuccessful trial and error methods for solving problems while under stress. I have observed doctoral candidates "go blank" when faced with questions for which they have prepared themselves well. Math students, under the pressure of a significant test, will repeat solution attempts they have already found to be incorrect. Victims of natural disasters have been known to persist in useless methods of self rescue, when a bit of insight might have produced a way of escape. So it seems to be with all of us. We are not in a position to see great insights or to achieve unusual spiritual comprehension in these moments.

One of my early and significant errors in counseling practice was pressing a client to come through with some insightful solution while he was still suffering from the initial blow of a problem. Likewise ministers and doctors sometimes crowd disoriented people toward abstract solutions to their problems before they are ready to think things through.

I recall, for example, a physician's attempt to explain to parents that their newborn child with Downe's syndrome (mongolism) would probably never develop normal mental capacities. He went through a great deal of accurate medical information and psychological data that would convince any uninvolved graduate student. But after about 20 minutes of careful instruction, the young mother, thoroughly devastated by the event, looked up at the doctor and inquired, "Don't you think he might turn out to be quite bright even though he's homely?" This young mother was a college teacher herself and it was obvious that her intellectual endowments had been well subdued.

The fact that people are stunned at impact explains why they sometimes make foolish decisions they would like to undo later. Consider the man who received an unusual job offer in another part of the country. He was so thrilled and disoriented he lost his financial awareness. Someone wanted to buy his house and struck a bargain with him that was well below the market value at the time. In fact the seller was two years recovering his losses from this and similar deals even though he doubled his salary by taking the new position. He had acted under the impact phase when his mind was preoccupied.

A young man owned a farm near a city. Following World War II the city expanded rapidly and his farm was purchased for the construction of a shopping center. He made a huge profit, but immediately plunged all his assets into speculative real estate ventures, thinking he could repeat his profitable experience. In 10 short days he was farther in debt than he dreamed he could possibly be. And in two years he had lost almost everything he owned.

Unfortunately, we often need to make a number of important decisions in the impact phase, when we are least able to do so effectively. This often occurs when the death of a spouse or family member has taken place. Often we must make major financial decisions at such a time. The number and seriousness of the decisions is increased in cases where the parties have done no estate planning and have not prepared a will. It is best for most of us to anticipate death realistically and prepare a plan that takes place automatically when we die. We may avoid great losses because the plan was made when we had our full rational capacities.

Search for a Lost Object

During the impact phase, when numbness and disorientation characterize intellectual processes, we also note a peculiar direction to thought processes. People actually and symbolically search for the lost object. Again, the loss of a spouse or family member best illustrates the matter. Perhaps you have noticed how the remaining family members will bring out all the photographs and memorabilia and put them on display. These objects symbolically replace the lost loved one.

When my grandparents immigrated to this country

they settled on a homestead in northern Minnesota. The soil was rocky, the winters cold, the farming poor. I once asked one of my professors of Swedish ancestry why my grandfather would go to all the difficulty of immigrating to this country and then settle on a rock pile where little would grow. I thought his answer was very perceptive. He first asked what part of Sweden my forebears had left. "Ah!" he said. "They settled in a place just like the place they left behind." They were searching for home —their lost object.

When we lose something important to us, we retain our emotional attachments for some time. It is very natural for us to keep searching for a similar object or replacement, especially when we are not too insightful about what is happening to us.

The symbolic search for the lost object is an important part of the grieving process. It should not be denied unless it lasts for a very long time. I remember a woman whose husband had died. She cherished him very much and was quite dependent upon him. When he died suddenly she was totally helpless for a long time. But before her grieving was complete she had found another man and married him. To his great surprise, she refused to move her first husband's clothes and pipe racks out of the house. The second husband found he was the substitute husband, and was expected to live out his wife's wishes for her first spouse. Needless to say, the marriage didn't last long.

When we lose something of great value to us, we reminisce about it during the impact phase of the crisis. For example, when our family moved across the country to a new home and job, we had to sell a nearly new boat we had come to enjoy very much. We promised ourselves we would replace it as soon as we were settled in our new home. So, one of my sons and I read all the ads in the paper for boats and we shopped and talked boats for many hours. But we never bought one. We discovered we were mostly reminiscing while severing our minds from an object we had come to appreciate very much. In our present situation we could hardly use such a boat. Delaying our decision proved to be valuable. We waited until reality was more clear and then decided not to replace the boat.

The most important service that can be given to someone in the impact phase of crisis or change is the simple acceptance of his feelings. Rejection of feelings only complicates the matter. It drives feelings underground where they are more difficult to accept and deal with. It is not necessary that all feelings be rationally sound at this point. The diminished intellectual functioning will often allow considerable irrationality.

I think of the example of Jesus at Lazarus' tomb. His feelings are reported in the shortest verse in the Bible. "Jesus wept" (John 11:35). Many of us would have told Jesus to calm down! After all, He knew He was about to raise Lazarus. The least He could do was not get everybody upset. But Jesus did not deny His own feelings. He expressed them and shared the full impact of human loss.

I think of a man who buried both his father and his brother in a period of a few weeks. They were very close as a family and were in a business partnership together. But in the name of Christian strength, he shed not a tear. He planned both funerals and conducted his family business as if no big event had taken place. I'm sure the grieving would have been much more healthy had he allowed himself to feel his loss. Instead he is now known as the melancholy farmer who seldom socializes and never smiles. He has only prolonged his grief by refusing his feelings.

One of the curious aspects of feelings in great change or crisis is the fact of ambivalence—highly mixed emotions that seem to make little sense. I knew a gracious old lady whose husband passed away while they were both in their eighties. He had been a grouch for some time. Someone in his church had offended him badly and he had held a grudge for years. He refused to attend the church where he held his membership, not willing to grace the congregation with his presence. Instead he grumbled his way to heaven and his death was at least a partial relief to his wife.

But she had great difficulty accepting the ambivalence she felt. She loved him and missed him. But she hated his grumbling and was glad he was gone. When she tried to express her mixed emotions to a close friend she got a jolting rebuke saying that she surely should not feel that way. As a result her guilt plagued her for several months until a wise pastor sensed something was wrong and ministered to her. He assured her that even Christ Himself had some mixed feelings. Remember His prayer as He faced the cross? "Father, if Thou art willing, remove this cup from Me; yet not My will, but Thine be done" (Luke 22:42).

The impact of great change, whether the change is positive or negative, will cause us considerable amounts of mixed feelings. This is normal, and the feelings will tend to work themselves out. We need not take on extra burdensome feelings.

One reason we find it hard to accept the feelings of others is that we become uncomfortable ourselves. I would like to have a dollar for every time I have heard a husband tell his wife not to cry during marriage counseling. The problem is that he feels ashamed to be moved by his wife's feelings—often feelings that are the result of his own insensitivity. We deny the feelings of others because we are protecting our own inability to be free with our emotions.

Since feelings often lie hidden beneath our immediate consciousness, we may not be aware of them for some time. When they do appear, either in ourselves or in others, our first impulse is to deny their existence or their expression. When others express feelings that bother us, our discomfort is a signal that these are emotions we need to turn loose, or at least we need to fully identify them to ourselves as our own. By not denying the feelings of others or our own feelings, we improve our chances of coming through life's changes and crises successfully.

Guilt

A word should be said specifically about the emotion of guilt since it so frequently accompanies the occurrence of change in our life. For example, a business organization employed a number of second-line executives who were capable of moving into top management. But they were all in the same department and it was clear that only one was going to get the top senior executive post when the boss retired.

The retirement came. After unusual care in the selection of a successor, a man was chosen. He was elated of course, but in a short time he was having trouble with guilt because he had deprived a respected colleague of the opportunity for the promotion. One of the other candidates had a handicapped child with accompanying huge medical and child care bills. The promotion would have helped him greatly. For a time, the successful candidate seemed apologetic about success, but eventually he learned to accept his good fortune.

The guilt of winning is seldom talked about, yet it is a common problem. One of our sons went through such an experience in his sophomore year in high school. His swimming team had won the league championship and now faced district and state finals. Each team could qualify two men for each event. Our son had developed well that year and had outperformed a senior who yearned to be in the district and state championships. It was the senior's last chance to do so, and only our son stood in the way of his success.

We talked about the matter at some length. As the critical time trials approached, our son went through agony, even thinking of doing less than his best so his friend and teammate could have this one last opportunity. We advised him to do his best and let the coach make the decision, shifting any guilt to him. Our son went on to the championships, encouraged and congratulated by the senior who lost to him, but who was a true team man. And our son's guilt was gone.

People in the near psychological vicinity of a crisis or change often feel guilt, too. One of the most troublesome aspects of divorce is the guilt of the children of the divorcing couple. Their guilt is largely irrational and unearned, but nevertheless the feeling is there. Inside they feel as if they are responsible for the breakup. Perhaps if they had not sided with one parent or the other . . . or perhaps if they had behaved better and not made mom and dad so mad . . . or maybe if they hadn't been so nice to the third party in the love triangle . . . maybe mom and dad would still be together.

Even irrational feelings should be allowed some expression. The irrational guilt of a divorcing couple's children is most often put down. Sometimes the parents do this because they can't stand any more guilt on top of their own. Or they recognize it as unreal and therefore feel they must deny the feelings. In either case, the children's feelings should be dealt with and not be driven underground, only to arise later in negative attitudes toward marriage or in a sour personality style.

Another example of guilt in the vicinity of a crisis is the feeling of survivors of accidents. "Why was it not me?" "Why didn't the other person, who is more talented and more worthy than I am, survive?" "Why did my child die?" Survivor guilt in wartime is perhaps the sharpest example of this. To have lived through some of war's terrors implies that you did not fight hard enough or you were ducking out when the battle was the fiercest. Again, such guilt is largely irrational, but must be dealt with openly rather than denied.

It is at this point that the difference between healthy Christians and all others comes sharply into focus. The Christian who has become familiar with forgiveness finds easier and quicker resolution to guilt, whether the guilt is true or imagined. This is because he has learned to believe a most important theological truth: God has provided forgiveness, whether we merit it or not, for all wrongdoing. God can and does remove all guilt from people. The reality of the fact is not in question to those who have believed that this is so. They have found freedom and release they could neither earn nor expect.

Since guilt is at the root of so many psychological problems, it is hard to estimate the impact that the truth of God's forgiveness might have on a race of people if it were taught and believed in childhood and became an essential part of the adjustment process through an entire lifetime. I suspect that if we could find a living example of a whole population for whom forgiveness was a vital part of psychological development, we would find a population with unusual health, happiness and release of human potential.

Unfortunately man would rather rationalize his way to guiltlessness or blame others or work off his faults by performing good deeds. By so doing he can play God in his own life, which after all is the ultimate sin. But when crisis arrives, and the tendency is strong to look within for the fault of it all, the person who is accustomed to seeking God and His grace is going to come through much more successfully.

four

Phase Two: Withdrawal-Confusion

At this point it might be helpful to present a picture of the emotions throughout the crisis and change sequence. You will note from the graph below that the emotions run high during the impact phase, then begin a downhill slide, recovering again as resolution is reached.

Change and Crisis Sequence[1]

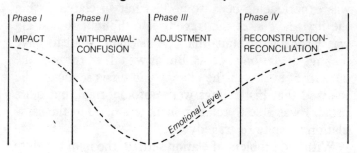

Phase I	Phase II	Phase III	Phase IV
IMPACT	WITHDRAWAL-CONFUSION	ADJUSTMENT	RECONSTRUCTION-RECONCILIATION

Emotional Level

The key characteristic of Phase Two is the decline in emotional level. The result is usually a state of depression or a worn-out feeling—reaching bottom with no more feeling to experience. Note also that each of the phases is a little longer than the preceding one. The period of impact is short, a matter of hours or days. The period of withdrawal-confusion lasts days and possibly weeks.

I once spoke at a family conference attended by a grandfather who had lost his favorite grandson six weeks previously. A careless teenage driver had run down the four-year-old lad in a parking lot of a supermarket. You can imagine the grief and anger of the boy's family, and the guilt the teenage driver must have felt.

All through the funeral and the days immediately following it, the grandfather was so involved in caring for his children, helping to make plans for services, and responding to bearers of sympathy that he was on an emotional high. In fact, he enjoyed the feeling. He felt more useful than he had in years. The continuing good wishes of friends lifted his emotions tremendously. But the downside of the hill finally came. Friends ceased their calls, the services were over. He was needed no longer and he desperately missed his grandson. Now he was "bottoming out."

One of the grandfather's concerns was the guilt he was experiencing because he had felt so elated during the first days after the tragedy. He thought something was wrong with him—that it was unchristian to have feelings of elation at crisis. But as we talked through the pattern of events in the change and crisis sequence, he realized that his feelings were not abnormal, but quite usual. I was able to relate how others had felt the same elation in spite of tragedy.

With the problem of elation settled, the man began to

tell of other feelings: intense hostility toward the teenager who had caused the accident, and anger at God for allowing such a terrible thing to happen. How could a God of justice allow the life of such a dear four-year-old to be snuffed out? But the matter of being angry at God rekindled his guilt. Now he was guilty for being angry with God. Christians are supposed to love God, not be angry with Him, he reasoned.

I was able to share with him the fact that anger is not uncommon on the downside of great change. I related to him my own feelings at the death of my father. He was only 66 years of age when he died, and I was just getting to know him in a new way—as a peer and not as a father. As a result we were having some interesting conversations. I was beginning to appreciate his counsel. But all was cut short with his death. I had hoped for a longer retirement for him but that was not to be. I found myself with angry feelings.

One noted psychiatrist has called the downside of change and crisis the opportunity for the "successful work of worry." By that he meant the chance to keep struggling until you hit bottom. He was a specialist in working with the terminally ill. I heard him say at a convention that those who have a chance to worry about death beforehand meet it the best. He was not speaking as a Christian, by any means, but had hit upon a psychological truth. The successful work of worry sweeps away the confusions and lets us know how to be dependent and decide whom to trust.

Denial of Feelings

The temptation to deny feelings is probably strongest in the withdrawal-confusion phase of the sequence. It is during this period that feelings can become the lowest and ugliest. We may be angry because of the loss of a loved one or at having been moved to another part of the country. We may have intense guilt for being so angry; or for having contributed to the grief we and those close to us are experiencing. Then a sense of shame may follow the guilt. The emotions are in the valley of the shadow of death. Then comes the temptation to suppress all these feelings right out of existence or deny that they exist at all.

I once knew a woman who buried both her father and an aunt within two weeks and shed not a tear. She had adopted the Christian stoic style. She refused to be moved by emotion because to do so was surely a sign of weakness. Somehow the idea that "power is perfected in weakness" (2 Cor. 12:9) never occurred to her. Today her life-style is one of Christian frenzy. She drives herself to a faster and faster pace and lives with pasted on smiles of plastic joy. She'll die young if she continues, still denying her grief.

The beauty of the Christian experience is that because we have no masks to paste on, we have only God's forgiveness and peace to enjoy. We don't need to deny any feelings. God knows us better than we do, so there is nothing to hide. We may alarm our friends once in awhile, but no gut reaction within us is unknown to God. And He doesn't scare easily or fall off His throne with worry about how our experiences are going to turn out.

We need to express our feelings during the withdrawal-confusion phase, and this implies the need for close friends to stand by us. Our social conventions provide better for the time of impact than for the withdrawal-confusion stage. At impact friends express sympathy, bring gifts, spend time with us, and help with routine tasks. But a few weeks later there are no such social mandates that bring people to our door. Yet here is the time when much help may be needed. Serious financial problems may be upon us. Problems of relocation, employment and even new social regulations accompany our change of status.

Even in the positive changes of life there is need for open discussion of the feelings on the downside of the experience. I've suggested to pastors that one of the best times for marriage counseling is about six months into the marriage. The downside has been reached, the realities have come home to roost. The romantic idealizations are gone and now some help may be needed more than ever before.

In the case of a job relocation, old friends have been lost, new ones not yet fully found. The newness of the new home is past, the deferences given to new children in school are completed and they are pretty much on their own. Again it is a time to be especially aware of the needs of those going through the downside of great change.

One of the tactics of those in the withdrawal-confusion phase of crisis and change is the tendency to bargain. Dr. Elizabeth Kubler-Ross makes much of this in her book *On Death and Dying.*[2] She identifies the phases of crisis as being: *Shock*—the impact phase we've been talking about. Then follows *Denial*—the rejection of the whole matter in somewhat irrational terms. Denial is followed by *Anger*—those hostile feelings we have talked about just previously. The comes *Bargaining.*

It has been said that there are no atheists in the foxholes in wartime. They are too busy bargaining with God for their lives and safety. We have also found that people faced with terminal illness often bargain for their continued existence. They may try to make a deal with God: "Let me live for just so many days and I'll make it up to you in service and clean living," they may say.

Or consider the business man facing a risky but possibly profitable deal. "See me through this one and I'll give you a healthy chunk of every dollar, God!" The fact that such bargains are seldom kept may be beside the point. The real point is that bargaining is one of the ways to keep struggling until you hit bottom.

I think bargaining is lessened for the mature Christian. As a result he gets to eventual resolution more quickly. He realizes that he lives in an economy of grace, not an economy of bartering. He has what he has by the grace of God. Therefore, if he loses something, that is also within the province of His grace. God owned it anyway.

But he also knows that really he is in no position to bargain with an almighty God. Keeping a bargain made with God is only repeating an atonement already accomplished. It is trying to earn what has already been freely given.

To complete the description given by Dr. Kubler-Ross, the final phases are *Depression*, then *Acceptance*. Those who can fully work through the cycle handle death and dying best. The Kubler-Ross phases have also been expressed as: Who, me? Not me! Why me? Yes, me. This colloquial description may be as useful as any.

Like the impact phase of crisis, the withdrawal-confusion phase is no time to crowd the victim to great spiritual and psychological insights. The anger, depression, and bargaining color the thought and prayer life too much. Instead this is a time to depend upon the resources the person has built over the years.

A good friend of mine was raised in a home where all conversation was in the Swedish language until the children went to public school. As an adult, he told us how he prayed his simple childhood prayers in Swedish when he was in trouble. It mattered not what the words said;

he retreated to his childhood sources of strength and let them be sufficient.

It is obvious that someone who has had no sound spiritual training is going to be at a loss at this point. The most desperate people in the world are those who face the huge changes accompanying modern living without knowing any good philosophical or spiritual reason for existence, and without knowing of the specific acts and graces of God in time of need.

Task-Oriented Guidance

If you want to help a person on the downside of a crisis, give him specific task-oriented guidance. Help him organize his day. Assist in arranging for appointments. See that he keeps the house in order and gets the meals and cleaning done. Usually the person experiences some paralysis of will, some discouragement; the simpler moves of everyday tasks prepare the way for full restoration of productive living. They are also a hedge against self-pity. Inactivity and self-pity all too often join up to prevent reconstruction.

Task-oriented guidance and activity also aid in the process of detachment from lost objects. Whether those losses are loved ones, jobs, locations, or status, a detaching from involvement and ownership must be accomplished. A widow can hardly stay married to a deceased husband. An employee can no longer fulfill a job he has lost, nor can he spend the money earned from a discontinued occupation. Detachment must take place.

Actually, the person going through change will probably adopt an approach-withdrawal method of detaching. He will approach and perform the tasks he must do, but then in quieter moments reminisce about how things used to be. He will approach new people and situations partly as fulfillment for things lost and partly as new objects. Then he'll retreat to wish and reminisce again.

But until the detachment process is nearly complete, a person who has lost a spouse should probably not marry again. The new spouse in this case will provoke reminiscences that may be uncomfortable. Also, the new spouse will find himself or herself trying to double for the lost loved one. No one can fulfill such expectancies, and the marriage will be endangered. A remarriage late in the detachment period, however, may have the effect of extinguishing the last of the reminiscences and can be a healthy factor in the readjustment process. However, a sound remarriage *usually* takes place in the fourth phase; reconstruction and reconciliation.

Notes

1. Adapted from "Crisis/Transition Sequence" chart by Ralph G. Hirschowitz, *Levinson Letter* (Cambridge: The Levinson Institute, Inc., n.d.), p.4.
2. Elizabeth Kubler-Ross, *On Death and Dying* (New York: Macmillan Co., 1969).

five

Phase Three:
Adjustment

A good friend of mine left a strong leadership position in a church denomination. He had done good work and many people highly respected and appreciated him. But time for refreshment had come. New ideas were needed and it was apparent that the leadership should change. My friend was first to recognize it. But he knew that leaving a post in which he had served so well for many years would be a traumatic event. Nevertheless he made the move. Following his departure he went through the crisis cycle. He gave up his attachments to things familiar and dear. Then he plunged into an emotional slide that made him a candidate for bitterness. But he refused that temptation and in a year found himself in a healthy emotional reconstruction that brought him a whole new ministry.

One evening we were discussing his occupational death and resurrection. He had just finished a series of seminars for older people living in a retirement center. A number of them were reconstructing their lives, and his seminars had been most effective. His hopefulness had given a new enthusiasm to the retirees.

He concluded his seminar with the thought, "Everyone should go through what we are experiencing at least once or twice in a lifetime. Then we would know how to trust and we could get untangled from all the things we think are so terribly important. For example, my leaving professional churchlife set my wife free to enter into a much expanded friendship witness. She lost all the obligations of return dinner engagements that beset her and consumed her time. She was able to get a part-time job. Most of all I found out I wasn't really essential to the life and death of the church after all. That idea of being indispensable had become a great burden—a needless one—and I had to be wrenched loose from my overestimate of my usefulness."

As is the case with most successful reconstructions, he cut short his own catharsis and grieving. I think that is *a most important signal* in the reconstruction process. It means that insight is again possible. It means that self-pity is not going to have a firm hold on the emotions and thought life. It means that the initiative for well-being has returned to the owner of the problem. While ministrations are still important, they are no longer the critical necessity they once were. The problem is clearly in the hands of the person with the problem and he is taking positive steps to solve it himself.

I recall a wheelchair patient, a man more mentally than physically disabled, who rose out of his chair one day because he had encountered a change of will. He had lost his wife in an automobile accident that was partly his fault. And he was unable to forgive himself for her death. As he grieved, he failed to eat properly and his attitude deteriorated severely. Aches and pains joined his problem so that eventually he was confined to his wheelchair.

Then a friend asked him to join a seminar to discuss the healing ministry of Jesus. He was reluctant, and groused about the effort it required to get ready, but his friend was insistent and dragged him along. During the discussions he discovered his own selfishness and refusal of forgiveness for his part in his wife's death. It was very difficult to give up his self-punishment, but it became clear that that was what he must do. He finally allowed himself to accept God's forgiveness, and healing began. His appetite returned, and strength along with it. One morning he hesitantly lifted himself out of his wheelchair; he has never returned to it. He has been reconstructed by grace and by a genuine belief that resurrection can follow death.

I have some doubt that the resurrection part of this man's recovery would have been so effective if he had not bottomed out and gone through a lengthy period of adjustment. It seemed he had to discover with certainty that he could not either punish himself or save himself. He needed an act of belief based upon the fact of a healing saviour to reconstruct his life. When we bear the guilt of failure and have no one to give it to, we can be crushed. When we rationalize our guilt, assuming that it is just human to fail, and get no external help the load can be crushing. But every man needs a saviour and then everything can change.

The emotional responses during the time of adjustment, or Phase Three, are hopeful. Positive attitudes begin. Vestiges of depression remain and return occasionally, but the outlook is turning upward. The key reponse is an expression of hope. The widow thinks of remarriage with a twinkle in her eye. The corporate executive talks again of the satisfaction of his work and his hobbies, after surviving an occupational plunge. The losing politician begins to construct another campaign with a better strategy in mind.

The person in the adjustment phase has nearly completed his detachment from lost objects, and begins to search for new objects. His present assets become psychologically more valuable than the assets lost in the crisis and change. The actual or real value may be less, but the psychological and emotional values are distinctly greater. If you are in close contact with the one making the adjustments, you need to recognize this fact. You can hinder progress by reminding the person that his present state, by some objective standard, is worse than his former state. It is the *subjective*, psychological evaluation that counts.

A faithful church member lost most of his property in the great depression of the 1930s. John suffered the crisis sequence and eventually was restored to happiness. Because he had been faithful to God and church he had committed substantial sums of money and property to charitable purposes. One day a friend was driving John around town and they observed a number of the properties John had lost. The friend was mourning the loss more than the victim.

Presently they came to a large building which our John had given to a hospital for extended care. "Just think," his friend commented, "that was once all yours."

Quickly John retorted, "That is all I have left!"

The subjective measurement of assets was the difference between them. The faithful church member could count spiritual and psychological assets that had survived the greatest of financial collapses.

56

The person in the adjustment phase is beginning to express hope. His outward spirits seem high, and so the ministrations of friends often cease. It appears that the victim is out of the woods. But those who know better will stay close and attend to the needs of support that still arise. During the time of adjustment, the public image of the crisis or change victim will appear entirely normal. He'll say he's doing fine, though he probably is still having some down moments. He *is* relatively fine considering what he's been through. But he still needs someone to be close, though not nearly as frequently as before.

The fact of the return of hope and positive expressions is a signal that the time for insight has returned. Until now it had been fairly useless to try to crowd new ideas or new spiritual or psychological insights into his mind. But with the lessening of tension, the person can be quite candid and objective about his state of mind. He is ready for an understanding of life in a new way.

I have a good friend whom I regard as an outstanding preacher and minister. Several years ago he was stricken with a disabling disease that completely baffled his doctors. He became worse as the days went by, and his family feared for his life. Through it all my friend went through the shock of facing the end of his existence. Then he had ample time to ask over and over again, "Why me, Lord?" He thought he still had much to do. But then he trusted God for whatever might come and experienced a sense of peace he had never before known in his entire life. About that time a specialist in internal medicine found a reference to his symptoms in a medical journal and hit upon the correct diagnosis and treatment. It took several months for a full recovery, but his joy at being returned to active ministry was boundless. Now as he reflects upon his illness he says, "I wouldn't give you a plug nickel for what I went through, but I also wouldn't take a million dollars for what I've learned."

Throughout his illness he had studied the Scriptures concerning suffering and people who suffer. He could come to no new conclusions theologically until he had experienced the depths of hopelessness. Then as his life began to reconstruct, he gained new insights, new appreciations and concepts that had never crossed his mind before. As a result his ability to minister to people in suffering and crisis has increased.

six

Phase Four: Reconstruction and Reconciliation

I spoke at a summer conference attended by a man who had just lost a $75,000-a-year-job. He had been a founder of the company that employed him, and owned a significant portion of its stock. But a takeover by another corporation through purchase of stocks made his company a subsidiary to a conglomerate. The conglomerate forced him out, replacing all the previous managers.

"What does that fellow know," he muttered as he heard me talk, "he's never lost a job." He was in very low spirits as we discussed the matter of crisis and change.

The same man appeared a year later at a similar conference. He was a changed human being. He was joking with everyone he met, bouncing from person to person, praising God and kicking up his heels like a spring lamb. When I asked him what had happened in his life, he chided, "You ought to know! God lives and it's one and one half years since I got fired. Remember that crisis sequence you discussed that I thought was baloney? Well, I'm on the other end of it this year!"

For seven months unemployment had hung heavy on my busy executive friend. He had fixed the screens and toaster about four times each and there was nothing left to fix, clean or polish around the house. So he started fixing his wife. Her styles were wrong, her housekeeping could be improved, she didn't read the Bible enough, and why couldn't she keep down expenses? "I admire my wife for putting up with me," he reflected. "She said she had married me for better or worse, but probably not for this worse. But she hung on and it all worked out."

Then a teaching job opened up in a junior college. It paid about one-fourth his former salary. Since he was well trained, with an advanced degree in business administration, he found that teaching was a stimulating if relatively low-paying occupation. Then he discovered that students were real live human beings to whom he could relate and who welcomed his practical and humorous approach. Furthermore he was able to help develop a group of Christian students that met regularly for study and prayer. He was on top of the world. "I spent 20 years in business and church activities just getting ready for this," he explained. "God had me and this opportunity in mind all the time. What a deal!" Reconstruction and reconciliation had been completed.

The key response of the person coming out of crisis is the spontaneous expression of hope. He is no longer wistfully hopeful that someday life will get better; he is genuinely confident and is making plans based upon his confidence. If he has believed valid theological premises his hope is sure and his crisis has probably been shortened.

Hope is the antithesis of self-pity. The two are incompatible mental roommates. Both are implicit belief statements. The man who hopes believes something positive. The self-pitier is a doubter. While suffering he uses his self-pity to gain attention, reinforcing the tendency to self-pity. Most of the people I know with enduring problems of emotional distress have made decisions to enter into the quagmire of self-pity. People recover from emotional problems more quickly when they decide consciously to cut short their self-pity. The person who is healing well emotionally sees that he must choose between hope and pity and that his choice is an expression of what he truly believes in his heart. So he participates actively in his own reconstruction, carrying the initiative for progress, brushing off those who would feel sorry for him.

Another key sign that reconstruction is going well is that reattachments are taking place. New persons are being chosen to replace lost ones. New jobs replace old ones. New homes become the places for new roots to go down. New spiritual wells are dug for sating thirsty souls. The scriptural phrase, "The old things passed away; behold, new things have come" (2 Cor. 5:17), seems to characterize more than religious life.

Along with reconstruction goes the need for *reconciliation*. This word has important meaning for the final phase of the sequence of coping. In normal human crises and changes, people around us get hurt. We are troublesome when we are in trouble. When we feel guilty we blame others. We are a downright inconvenience and problem to others when our lives are in tough situations. When we are able to enter the reconstruction phase, it is time for some reconciliation as well.

One way to initiate reconciliation is to do it symbolically. For example, someone you have hurt needs a helpful gesture from you. You can do him a favor, or invite him to dinner. It need not be a full working off of the private debt, for that is not a characteristic of a living theology of grace. But rather little symbolic acts serve as signals that reconciliation is desired, and these acts provide new psychological grounds for reestablished relationships.

Two women were close friends and members of the same church. Stresses arose in the church, leading eventually to its division. One friend went one way, one the other. One of the women was nearly physically ill with the hurt this problem created. With the division went implied accusations of wrongdoing and guilt. In time, both sensed the need for reconciliation. A simple symbolic act did the trick. The friends had not spoken to each other for a long while, but they happened to be having lunch in the same restaurant one day. One was just finishing as the other began. The former went to the cashier and paid for the other's lunch. The new psychological ground established between them opened the way for exchange of thank-yous and shortly after, that gesture was acknowledged and there was complete reestablishment of love between them.

No one goes through a problem alone. He takes bystanders with him. He unwittingly victimizes others as he goes along. Mostly he does not intend that it should be so, but under stress our human reactions can be pretty ugly normally. We are so busy acting defensively in our own behalf that we fail to see the wreckage around us. Thus the need for reconciliation. We may think we have lived according to our consciences but around us people are still getting hurt. As someone has said, "Everyone has the right to try to live up to the expectancies of his conscience—provided he repairs the damage he does."

A person's experiences in reconstruction and reconciliation are new to him, so he does something called reality testing. This phenomenon deserves to be identified because it explains some unusual behavior. It is a little like the experience of the newly converted man who is just getting into the newness of life with Christ. It is so new and so different, he wants to test its reality from time to time. So he may try to return to the decision making and thought processes he used before his conversion. He usually discovers that the new realities are so much more satisfying he leaves the old ways behind.

A person may test the genuineness of a reconciled relationship. The two friends who were reconciled after one paid the other's lunch bill, had such an experience. Sometime later they had agreed to attend a meeting together. But one of them forgot the correct time and showed up an hour late. The other was tempted to be upset, but soon found an apology greeting her. The reality of the reconciliation had been successfully tested. In the reconstruction phase be aware of the test cases that come up.

"The strife is o'er, the battle done, now is the song of victory sung; Alleluia!" So states the old seventeenth-century hymn and so concludes our experience with crisis. The final resolution is a breakthrough. New appreciations have been gained, new strengths acquired.

It can be shown that those who gain psychological strength and flexibility are those who have gone through stresses successfully while discovering new aptitudes and understandings in the process. For most, the changes that have been so difficult can become a reason for thanksgiving. Out of these experiences will come opportunities to minister to others in uniquely helpful ways. Someone has said, "Treasure your trials—after they are over." No one values a problem when he is in the middle of it, but many rejoice for the experiences they have been through.

Some of the most resilient personalities I know are seasoned missionaries. They have spent their lives in crisis and change. They have shifted homes, friends, institutions, cultures, and sources of psychological and spiritual reward. There are few grumblers among them. They have learned to observe God's progress in life every day and in firsthand terms. Several, in their old age, are still the most inspirational characters I know. They are constantly reading, keeping up-to-date on world events, interpreting the work of God in the world and thanking God for a useful life. Contrast their experience with some self-serving retirees who are living on the sunny beaches waiting to die, anesthetized by booze, and hoping their stock dividends don't run out. Without hope and without God. Off to hell in a Cadillac. They have spent their lives comforting themselves and now they face the great crisis of life without hope. The paradoxes of Scripture come to mind. In weakness we are made strong (see 1 Cor. 1:25; 2 Cor. 12:9). We are poor in possessions but rich in grace (see 2 Cor. 6:10). Thanks be to God who gives us victory through our Lord Jesus Christ.

Change and Crisis Sequence[1]

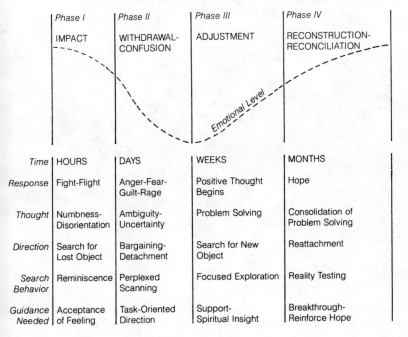

	Phase I IMPACT	Phase II WITHDRAWAL- CONFUSION	Phase III ADJUSTMENT	Phase IV RECONSTRUCTION- RECONCILIATION
Time	HOURS	DAYS	WEEKS	MONTHS
Response	Fight-Flight	Anger-Fear- Guilt-Rage	Positive Thought Begins	Hope
Thought	Numbness- Disorientation	Ambiguity- Uncertainty	Problem Solving	Consolidation of Problem Solving
Direction	Search for Lost Object	Bargaining- Detachment	Search for New Object	Reattachment
Search Behavior	Reminiscence	Perplexed Scanning	Focused Exploration	Reality Testing
Guidance Needed	Acceptance of Feeling	Task-Oriented Direction	Support- Spiritual Insight	Breakthrough- Reinforce Hope

Note

1. Based on a similar chart from Ralph Hirschowitz, in "Addendum," a special feature of the *Levinson Letter* (Cambridge: The Levinson Institute, Inc. n.d.), p.4.

seven

Crisis and Change in Conversion

Bill was a highly successful corporation lawyer. He specialized in working out intricate relationships between parent and subsidiary companies. Through his efforts his conglomerate had acquired several smaller companies at attractive prices and with considerable remuneration to himself. He enjoyed his wealth and corporate prestige, but the stress of his work was taking its toll. He spent long hours at work, smoked a lot, ate heavily to keep his energy up and began using the social drink to unwind at day's end.

Bill's formula worked for him for about fifteen years. But it wasn't working for his wife: her needs were not being met. She sought other social contacts. Unpleasant moments at home increased until the two led almost separate lives.

Bill's life-style also created some of its own demands. Once he sought the luncheon martini and evening scotch and soda as a means—they soothed his nerves; now he sought them as an "end." His body chemistry had become atuned to the anesthetic alcohol provided and it became a necessity, instead of a comforting luxury. The booze bills grew. Bill lost time at work because he was not feeling well. His weight increased with the calories of rich food and alcohol.

Bill was soon to face some tough choices. His wife confronted him with his problems and pointedly but carefully told him he could choose his life-style or his family. He also got a jolt from the corporate side of his life. His loss of efficiency had cost his company an important court case and he was on the carpet. Either he would straighten out his life, or his career was in jeopardy. No, they weren't going to fire him. They would demote him to routine tasks usually reserved for junior barristers. The thought of such humiliation was too much for Bill. He took the self-salvation plunge.

By sheer will power, Bill stopped his heavy smoking and overeating. In a year's time, he lost nearly 60 pounds and felt better than he had in years. He looked like a new man and his work efficiency improved. He was again trusted with the more important cases of law. His company congratulated him and assured him of a continuing fine future.

Bill solved half of his problem, the corporate side of his problem. But he was crankier than ever at home and he really couldn't lick the alcohol matter. He managed to keep off the sauce while at work, but he made up for it at home. More tense than ever, he doubled his consumption after work. His liquor cabinet was loaded and his sleep at night took place mostly on the sofa or the easy chair. By morning he would again put on the corporate success image and hike off to work. Bill knew it wouldn't last at work—his nights were too hard on him to allow him too many more good days.

At this point, two important interventions came to Bill's life. His wife joined a Bible study group and also began studying the problems of alcoholism. She, too, had reached the end of her limits to cope and was seeking anything that would offer hope. God responded with a small miracle in her life. She let Him take over and run her life which made her a new partner to Bill.

Instead of picking at him and complaining about his behavior, she began supporting his emotional needs and seeking ways to be of comfort. He responded sarcastically at first, thinking she was babying him or putting him down, but she kept on and he began to realize that something had changed in her life. But she was also confronting him. Not with moralizations about behavior but with questions about his purpose and hope in life. What was he really living for? Who was playing God—XYZ Corporation? Was his life truly the result of God's design for him?

Bill had been a church member many years. Nothing fanatic about it—he was proud of that fact. But God got passing attention on Sundays at least. Now his wife's questions were religious in nature and they were very real. Bill wasn't getting answers from his church. Why should they come now? They never had in the past.

Vacation time came in the midst of the questions and Bill thought this would be a chance to get away from everything for awhile—the problems and also the questions his wife was posing. Maybe, he thought, life would take a recess for two weeks and they could get a fresh perspective on things. But his wife had already anticipated his response. She had made reservations for the whole family at a camp in California, a couple of thousand miles away. Not just a woodsy, fishy, sleeping bag type of camp, but a Bible conference with several lectures a day, good music, good food, and care for the kids.

When Bill found out about it, he was livid. He thought his only hope for peace had been dashed. But his wife explained that the conference would deal with the most important things in her life since she had learned through the Bible study group to let God run her existence. So he condescendingly went along with the idea.

For Bill, camp was a bittersweet marvel for five days. He found himself faced squarely with the most important questions in his life. He also found himself living with his problems—those ugly beasts he hoped would stay home. But he heard some of the most outlandishly hopeful news he had ever heard. The news was of a solution, first to his spiritual needs, then to his personal needs. The sixth day brought the breakthrough. Bill quietly said, "God, or Jesus, whoever you are, you've got me. It can't be any worse than the way I'm headed, so you're on!" With that bit of resignation and the further discovery that the sins of the past could be absolutely buried by the grace of God, Bill set out on a new life. The last day of camp was one of simple yet bursting joy. Freedom and peace and love for his wife had returned.

Bill is a composite picture of a number of people I have met in recent years. He is 37 years of age, has two pre-teenage children, and is part of a group of young married couples that are a fast-growing population in many churches. He is young enough to make major changes in his life. He has lived long enough to assess his values and see if they are worth expending his life in their pursuit. He has tasted what life can offer in wealth, status, stress, and job satisfaction. He has built his life around the great American dream: education, profession, affluence and comfort. So far, he has clearly discovered, the deal has been worth less than the value of his soul.

Out of my observations of people like Bill, I would like to suggest that there are a number of important changes that come with a conversion experience like his. These experiences are overlapping, but seem to follow something of a sequential pattern. As Bill proceeded through this pattern, he experienced many of the emotions that typically characterize the pattern of crisis and change we noted in an earlier chapter. So many things are going to change in Bill's life that he will go through the phases of impact, confusion-withdrawal, adjustment, and reconstruction-reconciliation.

Some well-meaning friends will expect Bill to maintain his high spiritual experience and just keep rising from there. Most will overlook the fact that Bill marched to the beat of a different drummer for 37 years. It will take some time and will set up some stresses to get past his well-ingrained instincts and follow another beat. More than one young convert has become discouraged and fallen prey to well-meaning but not too helpful friends. Bill has become a new creature and is remodeling his life.

So if Bill seems to go into a downside phase of his conversion experience, wise guidance will be important to him. If you are Bill's friend or a member of his family, don't shame him or criticize his responses as he works things out. That he doesn't need!

If you review the list by Dr. Thomas Holmes in chapter 2 you can see quite a few changes that are ahead for Bill. He will see a change in marriage relationships, a change in life-style and habits of personal living. He may change jobs. He'll acquire new friends. Most important, and this item isn't even on the list, Bill will experience

71

a change in values. We are going to discuss four important changes Bill will experience.

Change in Relationships

The changes a new adult convert faces are sequential and overlapping. The first is the change in relationships with loved ones: husbands, wives, children, family members. These relationships often improve tremendously. For example, Bill discovered that God could forgive him, wash him clean and accept him just as he was. So he was inclined to do the same for those around him. His little differences with his wife were done away. He and she both sought forgiveness for past manipulations of each other's feelings. Then the kids were swept into the new feeling of reconciliation. New psychological ground was established on which to build yet further and deeper psychological contact between family members.

A unique aspect of the new relationships concerns the role played by the persons involved. Bill soon shifted from master to servant in his house. Instead of being "big daddy" who must always have his way, he began to seek out and consider the wishes of others. As he did so, family members granted him the parental authority he once had to argue for. His ministrations to family members were those of love and helpfulness and less those of command and dominance. In short, he changed from coercive to non-coercive methods of dealing with his close family members. Since coercion was no longer part of the family relational game, family members could be open about their needs and feelings and not feel that a put-down was coming for being honest about themselves.

We might note, in passing, a number of characteristics of an emotionally coercive person.

He wants you to solve your problems on his terms. Never mind how you feel, just come up with the right solution from a multiple-choice list—his list.

He hopes you will solve your problem sooner rather than later. He gets uncomfortable with lingering maladies. It makes him doubt his theology or his authority, or it just bothers him to find out that people are uncomfortably normal. He will shorten the time limits on you and crowd you to a solution you may not be ready or able to assimilate. He has little sense of the unrushed nature of the Holy Spirit.

He is judgmental in nature. He seems to think he is God's right-hand man in charge of handing down pronouncements about the moral worth of people around him. Most of his pronouncements are negative and demeaning, but it gives him a righteous kick.

He resists expressions of ambivalence. He can't stand the fact that on some days your Christian experience is downright troublesome or that sometime you aren't sure God is so great. Get with it single-mindedly and in a hurry, he prods. But the fact is that in any new experience, in any journey into new psychological territory, we are ambivalent. We approach and withdraw from our experience. We make feeble attempts at growth, then backtrack. For confirmation, witness Paul's statement beginning in Romans 7:14. Then remember that even Christ was ambivalent about the trip to the cross. God won't crowd you to emotional breakthroughs you aren't ready to handle. He understands, so grow clumsily if you will. Just keep growing.

He never quite accepts you as you are. He usually has one more step for you to climb, one more goal for you to achieve, one last failure to stick in your eye. Resist him and accept yourself as God accepts you—as if nothing had ever gone wrong.

Christians are not exempt from these coercive traits. Shortly after conversion, the new Christian will lose most of these tendencies. However he often slips back into them, sometimes with self-devised theological help. There are always a few Christians around who will beat you over the noggin with scriptural injunctions or home-made theological hammers.

Even though most of these coercive tendencies will disappear after Bill is converted, he will continue to need the power of the Holy Spirit to continue to grow in this newness.

Change of Life-Style

The second change that seems to occur in the new adult convert is the change of life-style. Your life-style includes several things: the way in which you present yourself to the public, your usual ways of spending your leisure time, the persons and activities you seek to satisfy your needs for play and entertainment, and your usual ways of relating emotionally to persons who are closest to you.

Since one's life-style is usually a public matter, the new convert is anxious to demonstrate his new life in Christ. He will therefore attempt to manifest this new life in visible ways. Likely as not, he will experience some internal conflicts since he is giving up some of his former sources of tension reduction and need gratification.

Look again at the Holmes list in chapter 2. If a new convert makes a number of significant life-style changes, he acquires a number of stress units as a result of his conversion. In the main, however, the new life will be more integrated and less neurotic. But the transition from old satisfiers and gratifiers to new ones is going to cause a few problems.

Earlier I indicated that an adult conversion has its downside phase, shortly after the time of impact. It is during this downside phase that the life-style problems tend to be most intense. One needs to remember that the downside phase—withdrawal-confusion—is part of the normal healing, adjusting process. The fact that life-style problems are seemingly most acute during this phase does not necessarily diminish the validity of one's salvation or impugn his spiritual life. It simply is a case of making desirable and difficult changes in life when emotional energies are waning. It is during this period that a whole lot of understanding and a lot less judgment and moralizing will keep the new pilgrim on the trail. He may revert from time to time, but he needs encouragement, not castigation.

It appears to me that we have limits to the degree and speed with which we can make fundamental changes in our lives. To insist on instant maturity, or sudden visible regeneration, as a symptom of healthy Christian life may serve to defeat the new believer. He may try to remanufacture more of his personal life than he is able to accomplish. There is such a thing as trying to grow faster than grace, and the results are usually negative. Too much failure occurs, a budding saint will be discouraged and may not try again.

Change in Values and Motives

The third change accompanying conversion is the change in values and motives. Consider Bill again. Just a few days before the conference that precipitated his conversion, he had gone into debt for a new, expensive luxury car. He was developing financial problems enough and did not need additional debt. But for Bill, it was exceedingly important to present himself to the public with all the symptoms of success. The new car was very much part of this syndrome, which also included top quality clothes, club memberships and the like.

With the great spiritual change in his life, Bill's values took a sharp turn. He was given a sense of adequacy and worth by the fact that God regarded him as His own son. He no longer needed to *prove* his worth by his success. One of the major readjustments that occurred about a year after Bill's conversion, was to sell some of his "adult toys" and reestablish his financial integrity. His values had clearly changed.

Bill's motives changed as well. Before he knew Christ, success in business meant acquiring the symptoms of wealth. With conversion his motive to succeed actually diminished for a time. Why spend energy accumulating junk? Is such effort worth one's life? Bill seemed lackadaisical for a number of months. But then he restyled his law practice and found he could serve the Lord through his work. He began to offer services to churches and charitable organizations. People in serious trouble or financial need found they could call on him for counsel. His practice became a ministry. He tithed generously, the Kingdom of God was advanced because of his work. His motives had clearly changed; he worked energetically again, because the results were of permanent value.

I have seen similar changes in others. A major university football team lost a significant part of its competitive drive because of the conversion of most of its first string members. These athletes had been getting their kicks and determining their self-worth by the degree of success they obtained on the football field. Then one by one they capitulated to the grace of God. They no longer needed the status and recognition athletics provided. They no longer valued the long hours spent breaking their bones and pulling their muscles. As a result they became a bunch of joyous losers on Saturday afternoons. The coach was dumbfounded, but he fully recognized that these kids had something he was still trying to find.

The apostle Paul declared that he did not even value his own life above his service to and for the glory of God (see Phil. 3:7-11). His values had changed to the degree that he was largely unconcerned about himself. Therein lies a degree of self-abandonment that frees one of virtually all concern, normal or neurotic. And that is ultimate liberation!

Change in Personality Organization

This leads us to the fourth phase or change as a result of conversion. As our relationships, values, and lifestyles have changed, our *personality organization* also changes. Becoming a Christian is not like joining another club, or taking up gardening, or entering into mystical experiences for kicks. It is an experience that fundamentally reorganizes one's whole life.

On one thing most personality theories agree: the central factor in behavior is serving the needs of the ego. Whatever reduces the stress of the individual, whatever feeds the psychological needs of the ego, whatever aggrandizes the image of the great "I," whatever enhances the psychological capacities of the person, that is what he will do. From Sigmund Freud to the existentialists and behaviorists, this one motive is recognized as common. Man is central to his own existence. The very idea that this need *not* be so is hardly recognized in psychological theory and literature. All religious experience and activity is regarded as fitting into orbit around the needs of the ego and its press for fulfillment.

I refer to this centrality of ego as *ego central* theory.

Very little theory has been formulated that does not start with this assumption. But when a genuine conversion has taken place this assumption comes up for a challenge. The writings of Scripture state the challenge for us. In fact the challenge is older than the theories—perhaps it is the theory that is challenging the psychological economy of God.

For example, the Scriptures tell us, "Seek first His kingdom, and His righteousness; and all these things shall be added to you" (Matt. 6:33). In Galatians 2:20 Paul says, "It is no longer I who live, but Christ lives in me." Paul also said, "If we live, we live for the Lord" (Rom. 14:8).

Paul was reorganized to such a degree that he was no longer particularly concerned about his own sanity. He wrote, "If we are beside ourselves, it is for God; if we are of sound mind, it is for you" (2 Cor. 5:13, *NASB*). In either case, sane or not, he had parted ownership with his own self to the degree that he was free of self-concerns. This could hardly be the case with ego in central position in one's personality organization. The most desirable place for ego is in orbital position—or the most valid theory must be ego-orbital theory, with the Lord Jesus Christ living in central position in human life and experience.

Obviously such a degree of change takes time. Paul himself was an adult convert. He declared clearly that the reorganization process had not been completed in him. This life was but an indication of things yet to come. But Paul could exult in joy even when the threats upon him were the greatest. It was while he was awaiting execution that he wrote Philippians 1. This passage is regarded by commentators and scholars as the loftiest expression of joy in any of Paul's writings. It suggests that either Paul lived a life in which self-concern was reduced to insignificance, or he was so deluded about his condition that he must have had schizoid tendencies. There is really very little middle ground in the matter. He was thoroughly regenerated or he was a bit screwy. And no screwy character ever illumined the minds and hearts of men as Paul did under the inspiration of the Holy Spirit. "If any man is in Christ, he is a new creature" (2 Cor. 5:17).

One of my tasks as a college president is to interview prospective faculty members for teaching positions. I have a couple of favorite questions I put to them: "What do you do for fun?" and, "What's your excuse for living?" The answers are widely varied and range from incoherent philosophy to succinct, exultant expression. One young academic replied, "Oh, I live for fun and to enjoy my tippling!" We didn't hire that person.

One of the signs of mature Christian life is the ability to state spontaneously a reason for one's own being or a reason for the hope that is within. When a future teacher can say to me that he lives for the glory of God and the joy of mankind without sounding like he's reading it from decayed sermon notes I know I have a good prospect for continued discussion.

When the mature years come in life I know of no greater satisfaction than to be able to say, "I know why I was made and what I am here for, and I gave it my best effort." The final change in conversion is the change in *reasons for one's existence.* Reasons that are sound enough that they surmount concerns for personal safety. Reasons that command certain directions in occupational choices. Reasons that are worth the investing of one's life and destiny. Reasons that bring glory to God and new life to man.

eight

Coping with Fear

The key emotion in any crisis or change situation is fear. Therefore, in considering the dynamics of change and crisis, we must discuss the emotion of fear. Outwardly fear seems like a simple reaction. Something comes to threaten us and we respond emotionally—we are afraid. Our safety is at stake, either physically or psychologically, so we feel fear. If we see we will narrowly miss an oncoming car on the highway, we pull away to avoid a crash. A moment later our hearts are jumping, we can hardly swallow. We are experiencing the physiological characteristics of fear.

Fears are common to everyone. You cannot find a person who has never feared. Several standard books on child psychology and development report that the most common fears of small children are dogs, darkness, and doctors. Most children have had physically or emotionally painful experiences with these three, and the result is fear. Sometimes just the thought of them produces tears.

Several years ago our family made an extended trip and found it necessary to take our cat with us. He is no little fellow; he looks more like a gray tiger. But his personality is nearly punchless so he is really no threat to anyone. One evening we stopped at a motel that allowed small tigers to be housed with their families. As we were getting unpacked, our cat took up a familiar perch on the window sill. Just a few minutes after he settled to his haunches we heard a shriek outside the motel door. We jumped to see what was happening and discovered a maid standing frozen before our window. Our sedentary tiger had yawned as she went by and scared the daylights out of her. We apologized and she then explained that ever since she was a small child she had had an irrational fear of cats, especially large ones. Try as she would, she could not conquer her fear. So when surprised by her most potent fear object she went into hysterics. Her fear response, which is a normal asset to most people, had become unusually keen and she lived with a handicap as a result.

Value of Fear

Fear is normal and should be highly valued. Fear keeps us from danger and mobilizes us when danger comes too close. Our hearts pump more quickly, adrenaline increases in our bloodstream, and we are capable of activities that require unusual strength and mental acuity. If fear, however, becomes the dominant theme of life, it wears us out and leads us to early physical collapse or even death. It is the abnormal fear, or the needlessly sustained fear, that should concern us. Be grateful that your heart jumps when you hear a siren, or when you walk too closely to a precipice.

A fear that continues for a long time and has infused itself into one's personality and life-style has two root characteristics. First, it involves physical manifestations —feelings in the gut, if you will. Second, it is part of an established perception and belief about the fear-provoking object. One must believe unconsciously or consciously that there is real danger associated with the object of fear. Attempts to change this belief have generally met with defeat, so that it persists in spite of attempts to relieve it.

For example, one may consciously know that small dogs are no real threat, but the unconscious mind believes the threat is there. So the fear will persist. It matters not whether the conscious or unconscious is involved, the threat felt by the person with the fear is real and should be respected. Suggesting that such fear is needless, or is just a mental quirk, helps little in alleviating such fear. We do not control our emotions well enough to easily put such fears out of our minds quickly.

When one goes through a crisis unsuccessfully, fears may take hold that dominate one's personality. Or if they don't actually dominate, they affect one's life so strongly that the evidences of fear manifest themselves in some significant way. Reckoning with the emotion of fear in crisis and change is therefore very important.

Fear is closely related to other emotions as well. While fear is usually thought of as a specific reaction to a specific stimulus, anxiety is a generalized fear for one's whole psychological well-being. Anxiety is an extension of fear into a pervasive general feeling. Anxiety manifests itself whether or not the objects that stimulated fear are present. The person with continual fear will become an anxious person in time.

Fear is also close to guilt. We have guilt because we fear. A young boy is taught in our culture not to be a "fraidy cat." If he manifests fear, he feels guilty because he has not upheld a cultural norm. In fact he may become the object of scorn of his peers if he continually shows fear.

The peer culture in elementary school years will often dictate that boys attempt some fear-provoking escapades to determine who among them is the bravest. I recall four youngsters who lived near a rock quarry. A trestle with narrow-gauge tracks extended from the normal surface of the ground out over a deep hole filled with water far into the quarry. The supreme test of courage in that community was to walk the narrow rails out over the quarry on the tracks. One misstep meant a 200-foot fall. Those who made it had special prestige envied by everyone but their mothers.

One little late-maturing lad had been suffering a great deal of harassment because of his fears of athletic contests. He was always running the wrong way with the football to avoid danger or ducking away from the pitch in a baseball game. The scorn of his peers became intolerable, and he was determined to show his courage in some way. He got together with the toughest kid in the neighborhood and the two went to test their courage on the trestle at the rock quarry. Slowly they stepped out, placing one foot after the other with great care. The little fellow preceded his tough companion. After great care and stress he reached the end and turned to receive the approval of his taunting friend. But his friend was not there. He had lost his footing and plunged silently to his death into the quarry. The little guy was frozen with fright and had to be rescued by the fire fighters, who had all too much familiarity with the tracks and trestle. The little lad has never been able to adjust to heights of any kind since. His courageous attempt had been lost in calamity.

Adults understand that trestles in rock quarries are to be avoided. But peer culture happens to be more powerful than adult admonitions, so the two boys were driven to test their courage. The fact that the test made no sense is pointless. Boys will do what they *feel* necessary more than what they *think* necessary. The boy who survived was driven by a need to avoid guilt because of his fear. The result was tragic. The story points up the relationship between fear and guilt as well as the fact that feelings take precedence over rational thinking in times of threat.

Fear and Hate

Fear is also related to the emotion of hate. The chances are that the boy on the trestle will learn to hate his fear. His fear led him to test his courage and he failed. His failure then led to hatred of the experience that made him look bad. People with well-developed hates in their lives are often troubled by a great deal of fear. Behind their hatred is the problem of unconquered fear. A man may hate his boss intensely because he has a fear of him that he cannot subdue or manage.

Similarly, a person who comes through a crisis badly is likely to have a great deal of resentment toward the things that brought about his problem. Therefore, much hate can be diverted by the successful management of crisis and change.

It is helpful for a person to know *why* he hates. If he can understand that hate comes from fear, if he can realize that he need not nourish his fear and the resultant hate, he will survive his life changes and crises better. Just knowing that he is vulnerable to developing hatred for the things he cannot resolve will help him short-circuit the development of these negative emotions.

The probabilities are that most people will go through life with some key problem unresolved. Some will understand this and will not permit the negative emotions to grow. Others will nourish their resentments with self-pity until they have distorted their personalities and become hating, hostile, difficult people.

Psychologists refer to fear, guilt, anxiety, and hate as the critical emotions. They are most devastating to the personality if they persist. We have pointed out the relationship among them here because they are easily provoked in crisis and change problems for most everyone. Furthermore they are mutually reinforcing. If fear is allowed to persist in time of crisis, it will tend to increase the possibility that the other critical emotions will take hold. If guilt is unresolved, it is likely that fear will continue longer than necessary. If guilt and fear persist they will convert to anxiety, which will become a state of apprehension that characterizes the personality.

While we have discussed fear, primarily, in this chapter, fear is but a part of the emotional package that results from a crisis or change situation. Fear is most often the initial emotion in any of life's convulsions, but it may not be the only one. It is therefore important that fear be dealt with as carefully as possible to avoid its reinforcing the other negative feelings.

The development of fear can be described in several ways. Following is a summary of four descriptions of that development.

Fear begins as a reaction to specific objects and events. It later becomes a generalized feeling unattached from its original stimulus. A child who has some bad experiences with dogs will be inclined to have a generalized fear of all animals if his first fear is not allayed. A child who has a hostile, domineering parent will be inclined to fear and distrust all authority figures. This could create obvious problems in employer-employee relationships, or in marriage.

Fear related to specific events and objects will develop into a life-style unless abated early. For example, a young woman became known as an unusually courageous person. She feared no height or difficult terrain, weather or deprivation. She developed these specific types of courage as a compensation for a great fear of insects and reptiles. Her courage translated into a life-style compensation for other fears she found impossible to master.

Fear moves from conscious to unconscious experience. If fear is too highly threatening we hide it from ourselves by relegating it to the unconscious mind. It is possible, therefore, for a very fearful person to have no sensation of a specific overwhelming fear—the sensation has been denied and exists only below conscious levels of experience. Instead the fear will be manifested symbolically. The fearful person may become a very compulsive keeper of records, or an unusually picky housekeeper, or a very orthodox, conforming believer in his theological and moral systems. These are symbolic ways of gaining control over life so that life will not provoke fear. Fearing people find it necessary to control others, through money, social restraints, or expressions of disapproval and the like.

Fear can move from specific reactions to belief systems. Unresolved fear can become an emotional force in developing political and theological beliefs. Political extremists of either right or left often have strong but hidden fear as a motivation for their needs to control and manipulate people. Strongly fearing people build rigid theological systems to protect themselves and sometimes to impose on others. The systems are the result of fear as much as they are of any inherent truth or logic.

Whenever fear moves very far from its specific stimulus, it is probably time for professional counsel. Perhaps the crisis or change is seriously affecting the life-style or belief system of the victim. If that is true or if the victim seems to be unusually oblivious to obvious fear objects, it would be well to consult with a therapist who can observe the symptoms and make sound recommendations.

For those without professional counsel, it might be helpful to know several techniques which can alleviate fear, particularly the fears of children. Youngsters are still pliable and can be aided by direct efforts. Adults require more insight and move less quickly toward resolving their negative feelings.

Change the Perception

The first technique is to change the perception of the fear-producing object. Most of us assume that a person or object that causes us to fear is taking an aggressive stance toward us. For example, a child who comes upon a loudly barking puppy may be startled and made afraid by the dog's bark. The child will easily assume that the dog is aggressively moving toward him to attack or threaten him. Usually this is not the case. Instead, the puppy is just protecting himself and his territory and giving warning that he is afraid of the approaching child. The child is a fear object for the dog and the dog is acting defensively by barking. If the child shrieks or cries, the child sees himself as defending against the threat of the dog. But the dog may assume the shriek is an aggressive threat.

Once we realize that the fear-provoking object or person is acting defensively, not aggressively, it is also important to know that our fear responses are probably being interpreted as aggressive gestures by the fear-producing object. When we learn to respond in a way that is not perceived as aggressive by the fear-producing object, the tension is reduced. We are less threatened; the fear-producing object is less threatened.

This phenomenon occurs in a variety of situations. For example, I remember a conflict that brewed between two small departments in a college. Each department was trying to enhance its status and its curriculum in a time when enrollments were declining. So each tried to offer attractive and interesting new courses to lure students. By chance both departments proposed a new course with approximately the same content; both even suggested the same textbook.

When the matter came to light, one department chairman became nearly enraged at the other. He saw the action of the other department as an attack upon his academic sovereignty. Fears immediately abounded. If one department offered its course, enrollment would be denied to the other. Jobs would be lost, security would vanish. The immediate and obvious solution? Counterattack! The next meeting of the college curriculum committee was a hair raiser, with representatives of both departments calling each other names and assuming each was out to get the other.

A wise dean, however, called the two chairmen together and carefully reviewed the situation. Each told his story as to how the idea for the course had arisen. When the facts came to light it was apparent that each had no aggressive or punitive motives toward the other. The matter was easily settled. An interdisciplinary course was offered, with both departments cooperating.

Fears subsided and both achieved their objectives.

When we understand that the object of our fear is acting to defend himself, rather than to attack us, our fears are alleviated. An example is seen in the conflicts of youngsters. Most fights between junior high schoolers begin when one assumes another is acting aggressively. The one so assuming then counterattacks. Very few fights are begun by aggressors who see themselves as aggressive. Most conflicts are begun by defenders who see themselves as counter-aggressive. As the saying goes, "The fight started when he hit me back!"

Studies of children who are described by their teachers as being very aggressive have shown that such children do not see themselves as aggressive. Rather, they perceive aggression against themselves in many more situations than they need to. Their aggressiveness is a symptom of a controlling perception that they are frequently under attack. The key to changing their aggressive behavior is to change their perception of others and the fear that such a perception brings. This may take some doing, for aggressive children have usually grown up in homes where threats are frequent and are solved by counterattacking.

Let's state the principle again. Most people who cause us fear by acting aggressively toward us are actually responding to some fear in themselves, and are acting counter-aggressively. When we realize this fact as truth, it becomes much easier for us to behave in ways that reduce their fear. When we are able to reduce their fear, they cease their aggressiveness and we lose much of our fear as well.

Enhance Self-Perception

A second way to reduce fear is to enhance your perception of yourself as adequate in relation to the fear. I remember watching a two-year-old boy's attempt to be friendly with a six-month-old boxer puppy. A six-month-old boxer is about the size of a pony and has a rambunctious nature. As the child approached the dog, the dog happily bounded toward the boy, thinking it was play time. He crashed into the little fellow and sent him rolling in the grass. The little guy was frozen with fear and went into a tantrum of helplessness. Father gathered up the boy and pulled him out of his difficulty. It was some time before the boy made any friendly attempts toward animals.

This boy's fears will subside as he becomes older. His relative size compared to dogs will change. Someday he'll be a big fellow and dogs will seem little and not so threatening. The simple factor of enhanced self-perception will reduce the fear. Increased size in comparison to boxer puppies will take most of the punch out of the childhood fears.

The boy and the boxer story is an illustration of changing relative physical size resulting in reduced fear. The same may be true of relative psychological size. I remember a young fellow and girl who came for counsel concerning their marriage plans. They were very much in love but the thought of marriage was particularly threatening to the young woman. She came from a family of poor economic means and little education. Most of her life had been spent in agricultural labor camps eking out a living by moving from harvest to harvest. The girl was the first in her family to get a college education. The boy was from a doctor's family where college was the normal achievement and where money was seldom a problem.

The fear that haunted the young woman was the difference she perceived in psychological size between herself and her background and the young man and his background. She truly believed that he was "too good" for her. She felt inadequate to meet the implied expectancies that marriage into a family like his would entail. To reduce her fear she had to decrease the differences in size between them. Or she had to find someone else who was not out of her class.

The young woman's first approach was to try to act as she thought a doctor's daughter might act. But that effort merely provoked laughter from the boy's family. She couldn't really play the part. Her perception of what she thought a doctor's daughter was like was erroneous in the first place, so her acting was based on misleading assumptions.

Her second attempt was to try to make a farm laborer's son out of her boyfriend. She criticized his fine clothes and persuaded him to dress like her family members. But he could not play that role either. His family reacted badly when he once presented himself to them as an "Okie." He also talked of dropping out of school to take a laboring job to make his prospective wife more comfortable psychologically. But it was easy to see that he would be dissatisfied with that lot as well.

The solution in this case was to terminate the relationship. It was difficult, of course, because they were genuinely attracted to each other and had conducted themselves toward each other in genuine Christian concern. The young woman has since married a man who became a teacher and works with rural children. The doctor's son went on to medical school and married a talented young woman who also became a physician. The two couples today are quite good friends and are thankful for the step they took.

The point is that serious differences between people in psychological size can be fear-producing. Sometimes psychological size difference bears little relationship to the real differences that might exist. But it is the *perceived* difference that must be dealt with. If perceived differences can be reduced, the accompanying fears can be reduced.

Sometimes the psychological size differences that cause fear can be reduced by acquiring a skill. A youngster who is taunted by his peers because of his insecurity can reduce the size differences by learning to hit a baseball well. Then he will find a place where he is equal to his peers. One boy who was poor in athletic capacities compensated by developing his interest and skills in political efforts. He eventually became student body president in his high school. His efforts had reduced the psychological size difference between him and his classmates, and his social fears subsided. Learning a skill had enhanced the boy's self-perception in relation to the demands upon him.

I have seen the same thing happen in adult life. I knew a man who had scraped along all his life diligently doing common labor. He was always short of money; therefore, economic fears haunted him day and night. But one perceptive and thoughtful rancher, recognizing the man's integrity, taught him to prune pear trees and to perform simple grafts. With this bit of skill available he soon found his sporadic employment replaced by steady work and considerably better rates of pay. His economic fears subsided as he faced the future with improved self-perception and increased psychological size. Again we see that fear is a function of the psychological size difference between us and the things we fear.

Familiarity with Feared Object

A third method of reducing fear is becoming familiar with the things we fear in safe circumstances. A college student told me recently that he feared two particular courses that were required for graduation; one was in English literature and the other in philosophy. He had heard that the English teacher was a powerful, overbearing type so he avoided him until the last moment. The philosophy class troubled him because he was unsure of his own ground in theology and was afraid he might be persuaded away from Christian faith. But the time came when he had to face both threats. He gathered his small bag of courage and enrolled in both courses. To his surprise and delight, he found that with careful preparation and attention in class, both courses were interesting and stimulating.

Instead of finding philosophy a threat, he learned the laws of logic, applied them to his Christian thought, and discovered they were a distinct help in sorting out his thinking. The student grew in his Christian experience even though the teacher had no such faith himself. The student's feelings of safety increased and his fears subsided as he became familiar with the fear objects.

Even if familiarity with fear objects establishes realistic fear, that will prove beneficial too. It is far better to face the truth about the feared object than to suffer fears of what one imagines about that object. The truly mature person takes accurate measure of the things that are greater than he, and then makes his adjustments accordingly.

It is important, however, to point out that familiarity with fear-producing stimuli must come in safe circumstances. It does little good to push someone out of the boat to teach him that shallow water is safe. Little is achieved by helping a child climb a tree and then leaving him to find his own way down. Such acts only reinforce fear. Familiarity with fear objects is a successful reducer of fear when there is certainty that an escape has been provided. If the boy who faced the bouncing boxer had become familiar with the dog while his father firmly held the pup, his fears would have been lessened. If the father had counseled the lad about the natural feistiness of boxers, the boy could have taken accurate account of the size of the threat he faced and adjusted accordingly.

Freedom to Approach and Withdraw

A fourth method of dealing with fear is to allow freedom to approach and withdraw from the things we fear. I was visiting in a home one Sunday afternoon after speaking in a church. My hosts had two small children who had attended the service that morning. They had seen me at a distance and now I was close at hand. They first peeked around the corners of doors to observe me and my actions. Then they began to run by and see if they dared to come close.

The next venture was to run up and take a quick look and see if it was safe to stop near where I was sitting. Then they crawled behind my chair and giggled awhile. When I put out my hand to touch one of them, they shrieked with fear and delight and ran out of the room. They soon interpreted my gesture as a friendly one and began to approach me again.

It wasn't long until I had both of them in my lap and could hardly put them down when dinner was served. But they illustrated an important point. When people have the freedom to approach and withdraw from fearful and unfamiliar objects, they adapt rather quickly and reduce their fears. The principle holds true whether you are facing snakes, financial commitments, potential marriage partners, or a righteous and loving God. We need the freedom to act out our ambivalence by approaching and withdrawing from the objects that concern us. If freedom is restricted, the ability to adjust is hampered.

Get Help

The fifth method of dealing with fear concerns us when we are faced with fears we cannot readily handle. Then we need help. We need someone to take over. When a paralyzing fear has beset us it is important that someone else be available to take over—to bail us out. These situations arise often in childhood and at the point of impact for adults in crisis. In childhood such events occur very frequently. When a child learns to walk, he is constantly finding his way into the street, into the lair of the neighbor's dog, and into the business of people who regard him as an intruder. In most of these situations he must have someone to remove him. He does not comprehend the consequences of his actions nor the fear he experiences when he runs afoul of these situations. It is also most important for the child not to be reprimanded for getting into situations he does not understand. If he learns to feel guilty for acting out his 18-month-old nature he will learn to feel inferior and frightened about life in general. It is better simply to remove him and give him sound friendly counsel about not returning to the situation.

For the adult who is at the impact phase of crisis, support is often the best approach. Removal is difficult in most adult situations. If a death has occurred, it is of little help to move away. It is best to have the presence of a friend and to remain in the situation. (If, however, the crisis is one of immediate physical danger, removal may be the best course of action.) In most crises, during the time of numbness and disorientation, a helpful friend who takes over management of the routines of living will be most useful in alleviating fear. It will be important to know, however, when to stop taking over. If the takeover lasts too long, the person in crisis will be limited in restoring himself to mastery of the situation.

One of the symptoms of overwhelming fear in a child is the tantrum. This behavior is usually regarded as the work of a spoiled child and is therefore ignored. But it is important to differentiate between the tantrum of a spoiled brat and the cries of an overwhelmed child. A child whose tantrum arises from overwhelming fear will be further hindered in emotional development if he is left to yelp his way through. On the other hand, the child who uses tantrums to get his way is aided in learning to control adults if he is *not* left to yelp his way through.

The important difference between the two tantrum types is the amount of psychological danger apparent in the situation. If the child is in completely familiar territory and is trying to gain attention or some toy, he is probably trying to control adults.

If he is in unfamiliar territory with strangers everywhere present, it is probably best to come to his aid. Likewise, if it can be determined that there is a real threat in his immediate presence, he should be aided. The point is that whether we are adults or children, when we are in trouble over our heads, the best help is immediate and direct support.

There are important biblical principles that can be brought to light concerning our dealing with fear. A key one is found in 1 John 4:18. The text reads: "There is no fear in love; but perfect love casts out fear, because fear involves punishment, and the one who fears is not perfected in love." The verses preceding this text carefully develop the fact that God is love and that He listens to us, understands us and lives in us.

But we often respond to God out of fear. We see that there are great differences in psychological size between ourselves and almighty God. But the amazing thing is that God has made Himself to be one of us in Jesus

Christ; one who lived with all the problems of life that we do. In this sense He has created a similarity between ourselves and Himself, and has reduced the kind of psychological size dimensions that cause us to fear. If we can further understand that God cares for us more fully and positively and knowingly than we care for ourselves, He becomes no threat at all, only Saviour and helper.

Our status as children of God also changes the degree of threat that any given object can produce. This is because there are no ultimate losses in the Kingdom of God. He has conquered all and will bring about final reconciliation among all things in heaven and on earth. Therefore, all losses we experience are temporary, never final. Knowing this helps us restrain our tendency to inflate the size or value of losses in life. We then have less fear to generate. Furthermore, the losses that hurt us have fairly short time limits on them. We have the built-in capacity to adjust to loss, plus the fact that no loss can outlive us. Our lives are eternal.

It is also helpful to know that Christ shares our feelings of ambivalence. We often interpret our ambivalences as lack of commitment or strength. But that is not necessarily the case. As Christ faced the cross, He fought with the experience of ambivalence as we saw earlier. He wished to go another way, but was willing to go the Father's way if necessary. "Not as I will, but as Thou wilt" (Matt. 26:39), He prayed. Similarly, as we saw, Paul discussed his mixed feelings about his venture with Christ. In Romans 7:15 he wrote, "For that which I am doing, I do not understand; for I am not practicing what I would like to do, but I am doing the very thing I hate." He had the same sort of inner conflict that you and I feel. In Romans 8 we have the assurance that such mixed feelings can be worked out and we can grow past our ambivalences. Verse 28 declares, "We know that God causes all things to work together for good to those who love God, to those who are called according to His purpose."

Whatever state of fear or crisis may befall us, we can be assured that there are no ultimate losses and that there is a regenerative work of God in all of our experience. In a time and in a world laden with fear and beset with tragedy, I know no better words to believe in than those.

nine

Coping with Conflict

I had just received my first appointment as a part-time teacher in a large university. Before beginning the first class I went to school a little early to check my mailbox and get the library lists in order. Since big institutions are somewhat cumbersome and bureaucratic, I went to the office of the department chairman for clues on how to avoid academic tangles. He shared an office with two other professors in a rejuvenated military barracks building. The other two professors were new appointees as well, and were also sorting out matters concerning their new assignment. But I found them locked in heated verbal combat. When I opened the door, they had reached the stage of name-calling, so I just stood for a minute to see how this hassle was going to come out.

The telephone was the apparent source of controversy. There was one phone for the department head and one for the two other professors. The great question seemed to be who was going to have the phone on his desk. One insisted that his desk was nearer the phone jack, so the instrument should obviously be placed on his desk. The other insisted that his particular teaching assignment required much more phoning so he should obviously have it on his desk. Each belittled the other's needs; and then the insults began. One referred to the other as an Obstreperous Nincompoop, Ph.D. and the other rationalized with a similar moniker. The name-calling solved nothing, so appeals were soon made by each to matters of rank and status. "I was appointed to my professorship before you were!" one shouted.

"But I outrank you in position. You're an assistant professor and I'm an associate professor. Therefore my wishes must prevail. Does not rank have its privileges?"

I'm not sure how they solved the matter, but the next time I visited the office both telephones were on the department head's desk. Maybe they went through the whole year without settling the silly matter. If so, they deserved the inconvenience for their childish behavior. You would think that well-educated people could get past such simple matters, but when pride is involved, people would rather die than lose.

Arnold Toynbee, the great British historian, has been credited with saying that man is astonishingly good at dealing with the physical world, and just as astonishingly bad at dealing with the human nature. Toynbee pointed out nothing new. That fact has been apparent since the fall of Adam in the garden of Eden. Any closely organized situation from marriage to government bureaucracy involves the needs of people and the tendency to act in one's own behalf in shortsighted ways. The result is conflict.

David Augsburger's book *Caring Enough to Confront*[1] is one of the more helpful books on conflict and its solutions. He points out that "conflict is natural, normal, and neutral. Conflict is neither good nor bad, right nor wrong. Conflict simply is. And how we view, approach and work through our differences does to a large extent determine our whole life pattern."

It is the purpose of this chapter to summarize the types and styles of conflict and to point up some insights concerning conflict in times of crisis and change. Let's begin by identifying two basic definitions of conflict: internal and external conflict. Then we'll proceed with three conflict styles.

Internal Conflict

The internal conflict lies within one person. The person has two strongly opposing needs, and these needs affect relationships with other people. In extreme cases the opposing needs can be so powerful that a neurotic personality develops. For example, I know a young man who had strong competing needs within him that grew out of his relationship with his father. The father was a well-known person and his son desired to be very much like him in a number of attributes. The father had been an outstanding athlete as a young man, and was a fairly competent pianist, a natural leader among his peers and a popular speaker. His son wanted to emulate his dad in most respects. But dad was also a very controlling and overly friendly personality. As a result he dominated his son in a friendly but intruding way. Whatever the son attempted to do, dad had to "help." Dad made sure everything came out right, letting the son take full credit for the achievement. But dad's marks were all over every accomplishment of his son. In time the son began to resist, then outwardly rebel. Father solved this by a friendly squashing of his son's rebellious behavior.

In time, the boy internalized the conflict. He could not outwardly resist his overhelping father so he resisted him inside his own mind. He fought for his own identity, but the things he had learned to do to obtain an identity were the same achievements that made his father well respected. So he was driven to achieve, but hated his achievements because they were so much like his dad's.

Eventually he began to fail, particularly in school. This was psychologically satisfying in that it made dad look bad. But it was also devastating because his own self-esteem took some awful knocks. The conflict within became heated—the need to defeat dad competing with the need to promote his own sense of self-worth. He could not do both, for the needs were mutually exclusive.

It will take some time and perhaps some counsel and insight to resolve the conflict. Dad is especially frustrated because he thinks he has the answer to his son's problems but can't get his solutions adopted. The more he helps his son the more he intrudes upon his life and the less his son is inclined to achieve. But dad doesn't see that and won't back away.

Sometimes conflict-ridden people precipitate a crisis and go through all the phases we described earlier in the book. The crisis may be unconsciously entered into; all outward appearances may be that some unfortunate event has chanced upon the victim. Sometimes the crisis may be a secondary event by which the person is trying neurotically to solve a primary problem. For example, illnesses frequently become secondary problems. I know of a woman who was a partner in a most unhappy marriage. Her husband was boorish and thoughtless. She could not change him and she would not leave her marriage for moral and theological reasons. To meet her needs for release from her overbearing husband she became ill. The illness was serious enough that much medical attention was required, but without clear diagnosis. Her behavior became more and more like that of a person who copes poorly. She became especially clinging in her dependency, yet often fought those who helped her the most. She wanted to stay sick at least long enough to enjoy a respite from her husband. Her condition of being ill and away from her husband was better to her than being well and living with him.

The internal conflict, as illustrated above, is usually more difficult to treat than the external conflict which we shall describe shortly. The internal conflict more often needs the skill of a trained therapist to recognize its dynamics and help resolve the struggle.

One of the interesting aspects of therapy for the internal conflict is the fact that the patient or client will use the therapist as one of the parties to the conflict. While the fight lies within, a sign that the conflict is being externalized is that the client begins to struggle with his therapist. The client identifies the therapist as his enemy or original adversary and acts out his conflict with him in a symbolic style. This calls for great skill on the part of the therapist. He must realize that his role is symbolic and not real, even though he catches all the emotional garbage the client can deliver. If the therapy is successful, the client will eventually realize what he is doing and will gain enough insight to prevent it from continuing.

External Conflict

The external conflict is simply a fight between two or more people. Each one has a need or aspiration to meet, and he sees the other as getting in the way of meeting these needs. The fight is not over competing impulses within the mind of one person, it is between the legitimate interests of two or more people.

Consider for example, the squabbles of children over the use of the family TV set. We have two young daughters with somewhat different interests who daily negotiate what is to be watched after the evening news. One likes situation comedies, the other prefers westerns. Each knows what the other wants. Opinions are strong and someone has to give in. So they argue awhile, then begin to trade. One will get her way on Tuesday, the other on Wednesday. As long as both win a share of the battles and don't insult each other in the process, the conflict is worked out. The resolution is never perfect, but each gets some satisfaction and realizes that fairness demands some yielding.

Sometimes we bring our internal conflicts with us to our external fights. This makes the external conflict seem much greater than it should be. It also confuses our opponents because they don't understand the internal involvements we are dealing with, so they may wonder what all the fuss is about.

I think of a husband and wife who had intense quarrels over furniture dusting. The husband wanted every surface mirror clean at all times. The wife felt that a once-a-week quick wipe with the polishing cloth was good enough. What the wife did not know was that her husband's mother had been a terrible housekeeper. He so wearied of litter and dust everywhere that he developed an urge to clean and straighten everything in his house. He then transferred this impulse to his own home and wife. His internal scrap with his mother added fuel to the argument with his wife.

Let's consider now, three styles of conflict resolution. These styles will apply whether the conflict is internal or external.

"I Win—You Lose"

The unilateral, authoritarian decision type of resolution is variously known as the "I win—you lose" method, the "I'll get him!" style, or the "I'm right, you're wrong, so I decide" approach to conflict resolution. The chief problem with this method is that it works! But only for a time. Because it seems to work for a time, the user is encouraged to use it again. With repeated use the weaknesses of the method becomes obvious.

I recall a family made up of elderly parents and seven adult children. It was an authoritarian family where dad made all the decisions. The adult offspring were all married and had left home and established their own paternalistic families. But the elderly father died suddenly. Mother was numb with shock and unable to move. She just sat and stared for several days. Obviously someone had to take charge of matters. So the eldest son stepped in, assumed his father's role and got things moving. The funeral was arranged, care for the mother was organized, and the estate was settled in a short time. It seemed as if all was going well.

But mother had never made a decision in her life and remained totally dependent upon her children. The burden of care fell upon the oldest son, since he had assumed the decider role at dad's death. But he was employed and extremely busy. So he ordered his wife to take hold of many of the details. She promptly complied, but when it became apparent that this was going to be a long-term arrangement she began to resent the solution imposed on her. Her husband began to *issue* orders to his brothers and sisters to help care for their mother. These orders were received resentfully and seldom carried out. Squabbles arose among the sons and daughters and in-laws.

Eventually the daughter-in-law who had been marshalled into caring for the elderly woman made her own unilateral, authoritarian decision. Either the old woman would be put into an institution and cared for there, or the daughter-in-law would leave the family and file for divorce.

In a few weeks the elderly mother went to a retirement home and died shortly afterwards. While her death caused grief, it made possible some restoration of relationship among the children. But many hurt feelings lingered that would never be fully alleviated.

This family problem illustrates the strengths and weaknesses of the unilateral, authoritarian decision-making method of solving conflicts. This method works best under the following conditions: first, when the time for action is extremely short and the correct action is quite obvious. Under such circumstances lengthy debate to obtain consensus will be defeating and the time for decision will be lost; second, when two conflicting parties are highly different in the knowledge or skill needed for an effective solution. In such cases, the most skilled or knowledgeable person can readily assume the right to decide upon a solution.

I remember seeing two men arguing fiercely about what to do for a seriously injured skier on a mountain slope. Along came a physician who took charge and solved the problem. Skill, not consensus, was the needed element in such a situation. But the physician's skill did not give him the right to continue to order the life of the skier. His right ended when the short-term need was met.

Obvious examples of effective authoritarian decisions are seen in parent-child conflicts involving specific skill and knowledge. Parents decide many things for their children because their experience has taught them a great deal. A father rightfully denies his 16-year-old

108

daughter the opportunity to spend a weekend at her college boyfriend's fraternity house in another state. A mother prevents her four-year-old from attempting to bake a pie without adult assistance. Adult knowledge and skill prevent calamities in both cases. But when differences in maturity no longer exist, attempts to make authoritarian decisions become counter-productive.

Unfortunately, some authoritarian personalities insist upon ordering the experience of others even in emotional aspects of life. But it is impossible to command someone to change his feelings or attitudes about another person. A parent who forces his children to express love and warmth when they hate each other is defeating any long-range hope of reconciliation. A forced solution inevitably brings conflict again to the same problem area.

A general rule would be that when a conflict concerns definite knowledge, skill, or information, there is room for authoritative input by those who possess such knowledge, skill, or information. But when the conflict concerns opinions, feelings, attitudes, or interpretations of motives and actions, the authoritarian method only produces more problems.

The key problem with the unilateral authoritarian "solution" is that it creates a winner and a loser. Thus we may call it the "I win—you lose" method. The winners in such situations begin believing that because they won, they were right. Because they were right they feel they should continue to impose their will upon others. But the losers are resentful and often don't really give in. They may grudgingly accept an imposed solution but will find ways to even the score.

An authoritarian business manager in a state university knew only one way to solve problems—his way.

Because he controlled the purse strings, he exercised the right to control all decisions related to money matters. If anyone opposed him, he assumed his colleague was insubordinate and should be put down.

Since the school in which he worked was a new one just being established, his decisive manner solved a lot of problems and got the institution off and rolling fairly rapidly. This of course reinforced his tendency to believe in his right to decide every question that came to his attention. But, in time, the faculty became resentful and began baiting him and setting up conflicts just to irritate him. In these contrived conflicts, which he could seldom clearly win, the faculty got its revenge. This points up a principle in conflict resolution. Conflicts unresolved or resolved by imposed solutions usually lead to additional, but symbolic, conflicts.

In the case of the state college business manager, the faculty set up an interesting symbolic conflict. In the conduct of college business it was sometimes necessary for faculty to operate state cars, vans and other vehicles. These vehicles used credit cards issued by gasoline stations that offered green trading stamps. Faculty members kept the green stamps for themselves. One day a scorching memo came from the business office ordering employees to turn in all green stamps to the business office. You can guess the response. No one cooperated. And the business manager was livid! The faculty had turned the tables and made him the loser instead of the winner he thought he should rightfully be. The faculty, with a sense of victory, expanded the conflict into other areas. Eventually the business manager resigned to accept other employment. He could not alter his style, and faculty resentment had grown to the point that routine business could not be conducted without great friction.

The fact that simple business matters also became

110

conflict-laden was an indication of the degree of serious-ness of the problem. When warring factions or persons inject conflict into even the mundane matters of life a serious breach has occurred. We find a similar phe-nomenon in marriage conflict. When a husband and wife fight over who gets to read the mail first, or who hangs towels on which rack, we conclude that these are sym-bolic conflicts in which the tension of more serious problems is being acted out. In simpler terms, when you can't win in one arena, you choose another. And the use of authoritarian methods to solve conflicts is the method most likely to encourage conflicts to move to new arenas.

So far we have talked about the authoritarian solution applied to the external type of conflict. But internal conflict may be subjected to the authoritarian solution as well. Since internal conflicts reside within a single individual it may seem strange that such a person should impose upon himself an authoritarian solution. But this is sometimes the case. The reason is quite logical. The person with an intense internal conflict probably got his problem by allowing an authoritarian parent to force an external problem upon him. He then internalized it and now deals with it just as his parent would, subjecting it to authoritarian solutions. The people I know who are toughest on themselves have usually had just such experiences. In extreme cases, self-punishment and guilt result from self-imposed authoritarian solutions. The guilt arises because the solutions are mostly unsuccess-ful, and that implies failure, and failure means guilt.

One means of alleviating such a conflict is to external-ize it and identify the original source of conflict. A few pages back we told about the wife and husband who argued bitterly over dusting furniture. His wife was the one who suggested that he was really fighting his mother when he argued with his wife. He at first resisted her suggestion, but as time went along, he began to see the truth of the insight. He then reduced the amount of stress he gave his wife over the matter because he could see that she was not the source of his problem. By uncovering the fact that he was reacting to his mother as well as his wife, he made an internal conflict an external matter and focused his problem more realistically. We externalize our problems when we get them out in the open and understand accurately who is really responsible for them. When this is done it sometimes renews a conflict between the person and his parent. Then the person must carefully decide if he really wants to involve the parent, who may be older and not able to work through the conflict again. Often in good therapy, the externalization can be accomplished without clobbering a parent who is not likely to understand what is going on and who will be greatly hurt by such a process.

But the fact remains that we do impose authoritarian decisions upon ourselves in our internal conflicts, or may have others impose such decisions upon them. The results too, are often the same as with authoritarian solutions to external conflicts. We become resentful, spread the conflict to new areas, experience a loser's mentality, and needlessly feel guilty.

"You Win—I Lose"

The permissive acceptance of another's demand, simply described, is an inversion of the "I win—you lose" method. It is the "Whatever you say, dear" solution, or the "You win—I lose" method. It is the acceptance *in advance* of the authoritarian, imposed solution. Like the "I win—you lose" solution, it creates a winner and a loser. But the winner also suffers because he is exposed to a false sense of reality. He really thinks he's right and that because he's right he gets to decide. But the loser, in permissively accepting the demand of another, withholds information that may make the winner's decision less than realistic. By agreeing in advance to lose, the loser does not marshal any forces or even offer any information that may bear upon the solution being offered. In the "I win—you lose" method at least the winner was faced with data that might be useful. Even though he may have rejected it, he did have to think about it. As a result, the imposed solution may be more realistic than in the "You win—I lose" method.

The fact that a party to conflict has agreed in advance to lose tells us something about the strength and character of the loser. It tells us that he has been beaten down so often and so well that his spirit is at a low ebb. It tells us that his confidence is shaken to the point that he has taken a "What's the use, anyway" attitude toward life.

It tells us that his sense of personal worth is declining and that he feels his psychological integrity is not worth fighting for. Furthermore, it tells us that he has little regard for the regenerative work of God in his life. If this method is continually applied the psychological and spiritual health of the individual is in question.

When a person solves his conflicts by this method it is apparent that he has avoided most external conflicts, and has internalized them instead of facing them. Avoiding all external conflicts is what makes this method attractive. Peace appears to reign. It looks as if most human relation problems have been solved. But inside, great resentment, guilt, and psychological self-abuse may be found.

In extreme cases the agreed loser may resort to self-destruction— suicide. Then the question arises in everyone's mind, "He got along so well with everyone! Why would he do a thing like this?" The absence of visible conflict is often a symptom of illness, not health. Absence of conflict is not necessarily peace, but often a case of buried hostility eating away at the one who has internalized it and pushed it out of sight.

When someone agrees in advance to lose in conflict, there is an additional subtle psychological nuance to be observed. The one losing has agreed to accept responsibility for the feelings of the winner. He has observed that when he loses, the conflict ceases, and peace returns. Thus he controls the situation by losing. But by controlling the situation, by accepting the responsibility for what happens, he loads upon himself a burden he cannot realistically bear. In a small way he plays the "suffering god" in the conflict relationship. Once he becomes the suffering god it is an easy step to suffer in righteous self-pity. Now we have the beginnings of theological rationalization for losing and the solution is all but out of reach for the emotional mess created.

As in dealing with all internal conflicts, externalizing the struggle is part of the therapy for a person in this situation. However, where the patient has agreed upon losing in advance, the therapy is more difficult. The patient must agree to two things; to stop agreeing to lose in advance, and then to fight constructively. If the therapy is successful the once sweet, peaceful loser will be seen as more testy and difficult to live with. But that's a sign of returning health. If the therapist must also fight the resistances of bad theology and self-pity, the probabilities of rescue are lessened.

At least one small lesson comes out of this. If you are a continual loser in the face of an authoritarian winner, at least don't let yourself agree in advance to lose. That is the abandonment of a vital part of your personal integrity that you dare not part with.

"Minimum Loss—Joint Gain"

The method that produces most hope is creative confronting and problem solving. But it takes work. It requires that the parties to conflict set aside some very important, though probably selfish, ideas to achieve a solution. We call it seeking "minimum loss— joint gain results."

In any conflict, people fight because they fear losses. The losses may be either psychological or material or both. In the opening illustration in this chapter we discussed two professors fighting over possession of a telephone. The material losses that the parties might have suffered were probably minimal. But the conflict soon moved to the psychological arena where human pride lives; there the possibility of loss always looms large. To have been defeated by another, to have someone impose his will upon you, is more devastating than material loss.

Recognizing that psychological loss is more painful than material loss is essential to understanding this method of solution. It is at this point that many attempts to solve conflicts go awry. Two toddlers were grappling for the same toy. They were locked in physical combat, screeching at each other with full volume. Then mother entered the arena. She simply asked whose the toy was. Both claimed it. Then she recalled that it belonged to one and not the other, grabbed it from both of them and returned it to its owner. One gloated in victory, the other cried in resentment and fury. There was a winner and a loser.

The material loss was not great. But the loser sincerely believed the toy was his. When mother imposed a winner-loser solution, she did not recognize nor respect the belief state of the loser. She made no attempt to explain ownership or the mistaken identity of the toy to the one who lost the fight. The result was bitterness and a belief in the loser that no one cared about the integrity of his perceptions. You can be sure that the same conflict will arise again, and that the loser will redouble his efforts to protect both his property and his ego next time.

Adults are not unlike this. I recall a woman who established herself in her small church as the resident mimeographer. The church could not afford paid staff, so she volunteered and temporarily solved a problem. Her work was a bit sticky and gooey, so the end products were less than first class. In time the church grew until it could afford a paid staff member to do the work, and hired such a person. But the volunteer mimeographer had taken the machine home with her and psychologically "owned the role" of printer. When the new, paid staff member called at the home to claim the machine a major church fight began. The problem was not so much the mimeograph machine, but the psychological loss of meaning and power exercised by the volunteer. In seeking a solution, no one recognized this loss; they dealt only with the problem of mimeography. The result was that the volunteer, who had been made a loser, withdrew her membership and friendship from the church.

In the solution to any real conflict, both the material and the emotional losses must be considered. A good solver of problems is also a good psychological cost accountant. When solutions are adopted, such a problem solver finds ways to compensate for *both* material and psychological losses.

The first step in creative confronting and problem solving is to identify the problem and the possible gains and losses for the parties involved, including the psychological losses. Two things are necessary to identify the conflict. The parties *must* agree to speak about the matter.

No conflict was ever readily solved in the presence of silent, withdrawing participants. The clam-up attitude only moves a conflict away from creative solutions and toward winner-loser solutions.

The second thing necessary for a creative solution is working through both the symbolic problems and the real problems. The symbolic problems are those usually precipitated by unsolved real problems. They are symbolic because they carry the psychological part of the conflict into new arenas without solving the real problem. Creative solutions involve psychological cost accounting. Ignoring symbolic problems hides the psychological price of solution.

For example, I have concluded that most serious marital conflicts eventually result in sexual problems. Since the sexual part of marriage is the most tender and delicate aspect of the relationship, it will reflect all the other unsolved problems of the marriage. A husband and wife who continually argue over child rearing methods and find no solutions will eventually act out their resistance to one another sexually. If one of the partners becomes a serious loser in the argument over child rearing methods, that partner is most likely to recede in the physical aspects of marriage. In order to solve either problem—the sexual one or the child rearing one—the couple will have to work on both together.

The third major step in creative solution to conflict is the abandonment of the "I must win" motive. Such abandonment does not imply in the least that one party must assume a loser's stance. But it does mean that both parties agree not to play sovereign lord over the other's life. This is perhaps the most difficult step to take. If a person has played god in his own life all of his years, he easily tends to play god wherever he can. If he has never relinquished control of his life to God, he is going to

117

resist giving up the "I must win" attitude. It is humanly normal and unregenerate to play god in our own lives and in as many other lives as we can. But to constructively solve conflicts in a Christian way is to let God do His own bidding in the lives of others as well as in ourselves.

The very way in which a person describes the conflict shows his position with regard to lordship over the other person's life. When one is still playing lord, he will be very testy about the way the elements of the conflict are described. He will insist on describing it in his own way, putting down his adversary's perceptions at nearly every point.

I remember a young lad, son of a business couple who were living in another country as representatives for a business firm. The boy had been in constant trouble with foreign authorities, and the family had finally been sent home to prevent further embarrassment to the firm. The family came to my office for counsel. I asked for a description of the problem. I suggested that the son speak first, for it seemed he was the central figure in the problem. He tried, but his mother would not let a single description stand. No statement was correct, no perception was accurate. After an hour of heated argument, I thought the boy would attack his mother to do her violence. I must admit, she probably had it coming. The point is that mother was going to have it her way; problem description, control of discussion, proper emotional expression, and finally, the solution. Mother was god, even though she spouted a most orthodox theology.

We were unsuccessful in getting Mother to yield on any point and after several heated interviews, she abandoned the counseling. The boy and his father continued, however, and achieved a beautiful reconciliation. Each respected the integrity of the other and refrained from controlling the other's feelings and perceptions. They left each other free to describe and feel as they would. Each one allowed the other freedom to propose solutions and to determine his course as he deemed best. In fact, as the discussions proceeded, each asked the other for more information and more expression of feeling so that every nuance of the problem would become known. This became a pleasant surprise to both of them, for they had spent much time previously putting down the other's input in any discussion.

The fourth step in creative solution finding is to work out several possible solutions. These alternatives should be placed in order of preference by the conflicting parties. The solution that looks best is tried first. If it fails, the second solution is attempted. If only one solution is attempted the party most adversely affected begins to see himself as the loser and without an exit from his losing position.

If more than one alternative is discussed, it becomes easier to account for the gains and losses that each party will experience. Then, according to the gains and losses estimated the participants can choose a solution that minimizes losses and emphasizes gains. They are more likely to be satisfied with the solution, and they have established a positive ground so that further conflicts can be similarly resolved. When each party senses that his needs have been expressed and accurately perceived, he is encouraged to confront constructively in the future.

The fifth step concerns evaluating the results of the solutions chosen. Sometimes an agreed solution works less well than anticipated. If so, an opportunity should be created to evaluate what is happening. If the evaluation shows that the gains are less than expected and the losses greater than hoped for, one of the other alternatives already established can be employed. Once again, the winner-loser situation has been avoided. A continuing relationship has been established and positive ground for proceeding has been established.

Note

1. David Augsburger, *Caring Enough to Confront* (Glendale, CA: Regal Books, 1973), p. 3.

ten

Coping with Stress

I'm sure you have some idea of what stress is. If you have ever been scared, had an auto accident, come close to failing a class in school, made your father angry, or been faced with giving a difficult public speech, you have experienced stress. Our lives are constantly ebbing and flowing with the feelings of stress. If you get too much of it for too long a time, you help out the undertaking business. If you live such a bland existence you never feel it, you will never achieve any real satisfaction in life. Stress is *both* necessary and dangerous. You need it, but too much of it can kill you.

The chances are good that if you have chosen to read this book you have experienced some significant stress that troubled you. So maybe it will be useful to discuss stress as a topic in itself. It should relate quite well to all that has gone before in the preceding chapters. This chapter contains statements about stress that are generally regarded as true today. But I would hasten to add that much is being learned about stress, and therefore you should keep an open mind about discoveries yet to be made. The human machine is fearfully made by God, and we are only beginning to understand it.

Stress Is Necessary

Any human achievement is accomplished under stress. Getting yourself through college, working successfully on a production line, racing in a swimming meet—all must be accompanied by some degree of stress. I've experienced some stress writing this book. At various points my thoughts were less clear than at others and my stress increased noticeably at those points. As I write this very line my daughter is playing her stereo a little beyond tolerance limits, and I am about to reduce my stress by asking her to turn it down—she has just responded favorably and I am relieved. Our relationship was not jeopardized by my request. But without some stresses this book won't get written. Stress experiences should lead to a happy conclusion. I believe that my life—and I hope yours—will be better because of the pains taken to write down these ideas.

Furthermore, stress is necessary to mobilize us to deal with the threats we face in daily life. The economy is sagging a bit just now, and that gives us a certain amount of stress. I am a director of a local bank and I sense the economic stresses upon the business community of our city. College enrollments are declining in this country, and since I direct the affairs of a college, I sometimes experience stress as I prepare to meet the changing enrollment picture. We may have to reduce our staff; that will be stressful, but will protect the economic viability of the school. If I had no stress over these matters I am sure that my effectiveness would be markedly reduced in meeting the challenges.

Sometimes God induces stress in our lives to refine our character and sweeten our spirits. Sometimes He gives us stress to display our human vulnerability so that His redemptive acts can be made known to others. That is good stress. We experience stress so His kingdom can advance.

Stress Has Physiological Components

The hormone of stress is adrenaline. When we are under stress adrenaline is being pumped into our bloodstream in greater amounts. Under these conditions we are stronger than usual and are physiologically mobilized for action. It has been said that two women can carry furniture out of a burning house that six men cannot carry back in. What's the difference? Adrenaline mobilizing the body's resources for emergency action. Under stress, hormones are released into the blood, activating the autonomic nervous system which in turn regulates blood pressure and controls the involuntary muscles, such as those that make up the heart.

In a *Mainliner* article, the physiological sequence of events was described as follows:

> Stress registers simultaneously in the neocortex, the highest and most advanced center of the brain, and in the limbic system the repository of our feelings. From there, messages flash along nerve cells to the hypothalamus, a tiny region of clustered cells deep within the brain that shape and color our feelings. The hypothalamus signals the nearby pituitary gland and the autonomic nervous system to begin secreting chemical messen-

gers. Epinephrine, better known as adrenaline, is pumped throughout the body; corticusteroid hormones flood from the outer layer of the adrenal glands; and the thyroid and pancreas release their stored hormones.

As a consequence of all this activity, the smooth muscles that line the blood vessels in the skin clamp shut, blanching the skin and sending the blood pressure soaring. The air passages in the nose and throat dilate, while the muscles of the stomach and intestines relax, stopping the digestive process. Cholesterol and fats are mobilized in the bloodstream. Heart rate and blood pressure go up dramatically. The pupils dilate and secretion of saliva abruptly comes to a halt. The spleen releases additional blood cells to carry oxygen to the tense and ready muscles in the arms and legs. The liver converts its store of glycogen into energy-yielding sugar, which pours into the bloodstream. The erector pili muscles contract, sending the smooth surface of the flesh into a mass of tiny bumps, a throwback to the days when our animal ancestors raised their hair to look more formidable when challenged.[1]

How one can be so sure about the animal ancestors escapes me, but aside from that the description seems to be an accurate account of what happens when we are under stress. The body mobilizes entirely to meet the challenge it faces.

Stress Can Be Addictive and Habitual

The experience of stress is somewhat like being on a "high" or a "kick." There is a bit of a thrill in being worked up in stress. The thrill generates a craving for more excitement, and stress is soon sought for its own sake. Why do people pick fights? Why do they run after fire engines and ambulances? Why do young hoodlums threaten others for no rational reason? One answer may be that they seek stress in order to be lifted out of otherwise meaningless and humdrum lives. But the problem is that you can become addicted to stress in excess forms. And excess stress can kill you.

As stress addicts seek stress they form the habits of stressful living. The addict learns to stay mobilized even though the direct need to do so has passed. He has mastered the art of keeping his adrenaline flowing. To break his habit he will have to return to duller forms of living and possibly go through mild withdrawal symptoms that form a depressive reaction and make him terribly uncomfortable.

Unfortunately some of us learn to interpret our personal significance according to the stress we experience. We start believing that the amount of stress we know is an indicator of how vital we are to the world. We convince ourselves that we are dealing with great questions and pivotal issues, and if we don't keep at it, the world will collapse. When things get a little dull, we have a ready repertoire of stress-inducing activities to toss into the organization we work for or the church we belong to. I have known professors whose sole contribution to the life of the academic community was to increase its stress. They were addicts, and the habit had to be fed.

Stress Is Selective
Stress seems to run higher in those who are seeking power over others than in those seeking to achieve something. For example, listening to a speech that arouses the need to feel powerful causes the listener to

secrete more adrenaline than does taking an IQ test which arouses the need to achieve.

Adrenaline flow appears to be low for people who experience the stress of grief. The flow is high, however, for people who are experiencing the stress of winning a political contest. Power seekers might reduce their stress by turning their attention to perfecting some trait within themselves.

Stress is related to one's capacity to solve a problem. There was a time when the giving of a public address caused me intense discomfort and stress. My skills were unrefined and I was treading in unfamiliar psychological territory. As my skills improved and my expectations for success were better adjusted to reality, my stress abated. I now carry on a speaking schedule that includes more than 100 addresses a year. It is still stressful, but only in a mild way, and is also somewhat addictive in its nature. If I don't do it for awhile, I miss the stimulation of such occasions.

Excess Stress Has Relationships to Physical Problems

At a conference of the Association for Research in Nervous and Mental Diseases 30 years ago the following were listed as correlates of excess stress: peptic ulcers, migraine headaches, hypertension, rheumatoid arthritis, backaches, emphysema, ulcerative colitis, neurodermatitis, asthma, cancer, heart attack, and mental disorder.

It is apparent that the human body and mind form a totality that must be kept entirely whole. It is no wonder that we so easily express total health as "getting it all together." Many people believe the possibility of achieving a whole mind, body, and soul is remote. But there is hope; as we learn to manage our lives better and recognize a total spiritual economy underlying our lives, we will be better people.

Unfortunately, many of the therapies applied to excess stress are useless if not harmful. The typical self-administered remedies are booze, yoga, practice of Eastern religions, transcendental meditation, and ingestion of psychoactive drugs. Some positive effects have been found to result from the various forms of meditation. At least one study reported that meditators returned to quiescent levels more quickly than non-meditators after going through experimentally induced stress. What is really needed, however, is a thorough application of the grace of God who forgives sin, reduces guilt, leaves us with a peace that passes all understanding and keeps our hearts and minds in Christ Jesus. That solution is the most hopeful and the one not yet tried on a mass scale.

Note

1. David Zimmerman, "Stress and How It Can Kill You," *Mainliner* (October, 1976), pp. 31-33.

eleven

People Who Cope Poorly in Crisis

In our city lived a closely knit family; elderly parents and two sons, Fred and Jack, both married. They all lived within a few blocks of each other and saw each other frequently. As the parents grew older and required more care, it fell to the sons to provide increasing assistance. Fred and Jack spent a lot of time assisting in meal preparation, house repairs, laundry and the like. Soon the demands were beginning to wear on Fred particularly, and he began to shun his responsibilities to his parents. This left Jack to assume even more of the burden.

In time, the father suffered a stroke and was completely helpless. At the time of the incident only Fred was home. But for several days he dug in and helped nobly until Jack, who was out of town, could be notified and returned home. At that point, Fred quickly escaped further involvement, had his telephone disconnected and managed to disappear from every family scene and to avoid any request for help.

This withdrawal from helpfulness provided fuel for a heated argument between the brothers. But the conflict produced no happy results. It became impossible to involve Fred, who ran away from the stress. Jack was forced to pick up the entire load, both financially and in caring activity.

A quick review of Fred's life would reveal some reasons for his withdrawal. He had had a most unfortunate military experience. He had suffered through a questionably just court-martial following a harrowing battle experience. As a teenager he was nearly declared guilty of reckless driving in a fatal automobile accident. He required hospitalization for emotional exhaustion for some weeks following the trial. As a child he had been unfavorably compared to his brother, who was distinctly more academic and athletic than he. In short, he had been nearly overwhelmed in crises a number of times before.

When Fred disconnected his phone, he limited the amount of stress that could reach him. To be sure, it set up other stresses with his family. But to his mind this was the most feasible way to manage his feelings.

There are several characteristics of people who cope poorly in crisis: They have been overwhelmed previously in stress situations; they may be in poor physical condition; they oversimplify problems into an underestmate of their realities; they respond to symptoms—fail to come to terms with causal factors in the problem; they resort to "magic of the mouth"—excessive eating, smoking, drinking, gabbing; they crowd time dimensions or extend them beyond useful limits; they experience a high "shame tax"; they shift from *what* is the problem to *who* is the problem; they are excessively independent or excessively clinging and dependent; they resist ministrations of people who can truly help; they have little or no certain and working theology; they suffer from ownership of self.

Emotional Problems Limit Copeability

The first characteristic of people who cope poorly in crisis is that they are nearly overwhelmed in crises. Then when they are under pressure they must make the most psychologically economic adjustments that they can devise. We may feel quite sure that more useful or productive approaches could be made. But from the viewpoint of the person with the problem, his adaptation will be the most efficient thing he can do, emotionally. If he has been overwhelmed previously, his adjustment may seem poor and inefficient to us, but for him, it will be the best move he can make under the conditions as he sees them.

The same principle holds true for the person who is mentally ill. Even the bizarre symptoms manifested by a schizophrenic should be regarded as the best moves that person can make under the circumstances. It does no good whatever, only harm, to ask a dissociated person to make a more reasonable adjustment—more reasonable by our standards.

Poor Physical Condition

The second characteristic of those who cope poorly in crisis is the possibility of poor physical condition. No lingering psychological problem is free from physical involvements and impairments. Those stubborn problems that seem to escape the aid of insight and emotional support most often have important physical, biological involvements. Every act of behavior, including thought processes, involves the use of some body tissue. And if the delicate balances of body chemistry and biology are upset, or if the physical resources are exhausted, crisis will overwhelm.

I worked with a college girl who struggled both for grades and for personal stability in her first years of college. She once went through a strange episode where she stood up in class and began a bizarre lecture in the midst of the professor's teaching. When she was referred for a psychiatric workup, it was discovered that she had a serious hypoglycemic condition that affected her mental balance. Medical help was the answer. In a few weeks she returned to class with normal responses. Her personal crisis had been precipitated by a physical problem.

Whenever poor coping appears during a serious problem it is absolutely vital to obtain a good physical examination to determine a possible source of the adjustment problems.

Denial of Reality

We recently watched a television program concerning the work of a young woman physician who was a resident in a treatment program for cancer victims. During the course of the residency, the young doctor discovered that she, too, had symptoms of cancer. She had a lump in her breast, but she ignored it. In fact, the more she worked with her patients and saw their problems the more she was inclined to deny the reality of her own condition. But during casual conversation with a fellow physician she mentioned the matter. Her peer immediately pressed the matter to see if she was doing anything about it. When she discovered that the other physician was denying reality, she took matters into her own hands and arranged for a biopsy and subsequent surgery.

By the narrowest of time limits, the life of the young physician was spared.

It seems highly unlikely that a physician would deny the reality of her own condition. But we know that thousands of people die annually because of the denial of similar realities. It is one of the characteristics of persons who cope poorly in crisis. I have seen educated, professional people who refuse to believe that they have a mentally handicapped child. Others refuse to face the fact that a financial crisis may be upon them. I observed the closing of a business operated by two brothers who had to be carried out of their shop by sheriff's deputies because they denied the reality of their bankruptcy. The denial of reality is a psychological move to avoid pain, anger, and all the emotions that go with the impact and the following emotional slide that accompany crisis.

Failure to Come to Terms

Yet another characteristic of those who cope poorly is the failure to come to terms with the problems. The person responds to the symptoms rather than the causes. I remember a hyperactive sixth grader who was so tense and wiggly he could scarcely concentrate on school work. Gradually he learned to upset and control the teaching process in his classroom. He could, by inappropriate behavior, keep anything academic from happening. If other children cooperated with the teacher, he harassed them at recess until they too resisted all instructional efforts.

In my review of the case, I discovered that the boy was somewhat below average in mental ability, but had parents who aspired highly for him. They were determined that he would finish law school some day, in the tradition of his father and two previous generations. As we discussed the matter, I found that the parents were most anxious to have me counsel the boy about his misbehavior in school and about his nervousness which was becoming a problem at home.

When I tried to get at causes, such as the lack of native intelligence, father and mother became angry with me. They immediately rationalized that I was part of a system that was responsible for the deteriorating quality of schooling. They appeared at a school board meeting one evening to make the most of our mismanagement of their child's education. In short, they were more interested in dealing with the symptoms surrounding the problem, than in the problem itself. They were determined to live vicariously in their child, and his limited mental capacity was not going to stand in their way. This preoccupation with symptoms is a denial of the reality of the problem, as mentioned earlier. By focusing on symptoms, the mind's attention is drawn away from the real problem that is too uncomfortable to face.

"Magic of the Mouth"

Dr. Ralph Hirschowitz, Harvard psychiatrist, has coined the term "magic of the mouth" to describe the next characteristic of those who cope poorly in crisis and change. By "magic of the mouth" we mean the tendency to eat, drink, smoke, and gab excessively. It may be a form of regression to infantile forms of behavior that takes hold when trouble comes to the poorly prepared. Remember Bill, the attorney who was converted? He had several of these "magic of the mouth" symptoms. He took to heavy smoking and drinking and gained much excess weight. He was uncomfortable unless he was putting something in his mouth almost all of the time.

There is a satisfaction in resorting to the magic of the

mouth, but it also creates problems. Then, instead of having one problem to deal with, you have two. The verbal catharsis of constant gabbing can become a habit that will continue even after the crisis is past. So it is with food, drink or smoking. A successful resolution for the problem at hand may be found, but the problems that resulted from inadequate coping attempts will have to be dealt with, too.

Unrealistic Approach to Time

The next characteristic of poor copers is an unrealistic approach to time. Like the emotionally coercive people we discussed earlier, poor copers will crowd the time dimensions of a problem. Or they may take the opposite approach and extend the time factors beyond all useful limits. Poor copers like instantaneous solutions, or they like to fiddle around while Rome burns. Extending time limits unreasonably is a way of denying the reality of the problems by postponing them. This avoids the discomfort of reality, but the eventual reality is likely to be crushing. It's a bit like a neglected dental examination. The examination may inflict pain by dealing with reality. It seems easier to postpone the whole miserable process, but when you do get around to it you may have lost your teeth. In that case the "solution" has been tougher than the problem.

"Shame Tax"

Another characteristic of the person who copes poorly can be illustrated by the story of a young wife I met a few years ago. She had grown up in a pious home, where parents showed considerable anxiety about her behavior. Each supper time began with a prayer for the meal about to be served, a prayer that ended with her parents confessing all of her sins for the day. Her earliest remembrances of family life concerned these confessions. As a result, she grew up believing herself to be a shameful person, unworthy of anyone's care. In adulthood she struggled constantly to generate a sense of self-adequacy, but without much success. Eventually, she found even the routine tasks of daily living overwhelming. So much shame had been poured out upon her that her emotional life had been demolished.

This young woman had spent her life paying a "shame tax" that was needlessly imposed. Such is the experience of many people who find themselves unable to master normal expectancies of life. Someone has imposed the shame tax upon them, making them pay an unusual emotional price for their peace of mind.

Imposing the shame tax is a common social phenomenon. One of the ways a society deals with its gnawing problems is to blame the victim. In our society this is a common dodge to avoid facing some of our most difficult problems. We blame the poor for not working hard enough. We blame the criminal for not being moral enough, or the emotionally sick person for bringing on his own problem. So we also treat crisis victims with blame or shame for having a problem.

But the fact is that imposing shame or guilt on a victim of a great change or crisis only complicates his situation. I recall a man who had been in a serious auto accident. He was driving late at night and was struck by another driver who had fallen asleep at the wheel. But the victim's wife complicated his rehabiliation by constantly reminding her husband that if he hadn't been out late, or had stopped at a motel instead of trying to drive late, he would not have been in the accident. It was virtually impossible to get the woman to stop nagging her suffering husband. But he found a rather direct way of dealing with his thoughtless wife. He clubbed her across the shins with a broomstick and told her that if she mentioned what he should have done one more time she'd get another wallop. She got the message, and his recovery appeared to be much speeded.

The shame tax is easily imposed in a number of problems. Examples include the young woman who becomes pregnant out of wedlock, the young driver who needlessly wrecks his car, the person who makes an obviously bad financial agreement in a moment of weakness. Most of us have highly developed "senses of ought." We already know how to behave better than we do. In fact we are so "ought conscious" we have hardly any peace about anything we do in this complicated society. To add a shame tax to an overworked sense of ought can become the crowning blow in a struggle to manage one's problems. So we don't manage them.

Shift from "What" to "Who"

We further find that the crisis victim who copes poorly shifts easily from *what* is the problem to *who* is the problem. Instead of focusing objectively upon causes of his problem he will personalize the dilemma and begin to seek persons to blame. I remember a teacher who had great difficulty putting on an adequate program in his classroom. Since the teacher shortage was with us at this time, the school district reluctantly rehired him for several years in a row. But then a new supervisor decided that enough was enough and recommended that tenure not be granted. The teacher received notice in March that his contract would expire the following June when school closed.

The man's method of dealing with the crisis was to search out enemies, real and imagined, and try to fix blame for his fate upon them. He paid no attention to the teaching problems he was having for he had convinced himself that he was a successful educator. As a result he completely missed the opportunity to make useful corrections and adjustments. He turned away those who might have helped him. He shifted from *what* was the problem to *who* was the problem and deceived himself. He ended his teaching career with an angry letter to the board of trustees denouncing all those who had conspired against him and had destroyed what he believed to be a promising career.

Dependency Problems

An additional characteristic of the person who copes poorly is the tendency to be either very independent or very dependent. He will cling excessively, or he will turn away from all those who might be of help. No doubt you have seen examples of both types of adjustment.

A college girl became pregnant out of wedlock. In her great desire for love and security she had compromised some very important values. When she became aware of her condition she promptly attached herself emotionally to us. We could hardly breathe or move without affecting her in some way. It became our task to help secure medical help and to work out relationships with her parents. They were shocked, but not too helpful. Her parents had not learned to cope very well with problems themselves. Eventually the young woman bore a healthy child and placed him in a Christian home. Through the counsel of a caring social worker, she made a successful reentry to normal living and eventually enjoyed a happy marriage.

Perhaps you have also witnessed the individual who avoids all help in time of crisis. I know of a family that experienced two deaths in a short period of time. The father died suddenly while working on the family farm, and a few weeks later one of his sons also died. The confusion was almost unbelievable. The father and two sons were in a partnership in a large farming venture. The partnership lacked a sound legal basis, and both father and son died without wills or adequate estate plans. The rush of creditors, bill collectors, and salesmen almost demolished the stability of the remaining family members. It was apparent that some straightforward legal advice could have saved untold financial grief. But their habit was to consult nobody. God would provide, they reasoned. But God also provides ministers of all sorts, including attorneys, and these people resisted all forms of ministration. The end result was bankruptcy and a crash from well-to-do status to complete economic dependency for the remaining family members.

No Workable Theology

There are two final characteristics of those who cope poorly in change and crisis. Both are theological and spiritual in nature. The first is the fact that the poor coper often has no certain, workable theology to see him through his troubles. He believes nothing that comforts him, nothing that adjusts his values for him, nothing that gives him hopeful perspective on his problem.

I have tried to help those whose theology is totally dependent upon their glands. God seems to retreat every time they need a tranquilizer. Every headache is the devil working up a storm. Their God is no more than a wishy-washy character who shows up only for chorus singing time, church smorgasbords, or an occasional koinonia meeting. A person without a workable theology—a knowledge of God—is ill-prepared to cope when a tumultuous world breaks over his head.

It has been my privilege from time to time to counsel with Christians from churches that have emphasized the sovereignty and caring nature of God. Thoroughly imbued with a trust in the providence of God, they have been reinforced for the day when trouble comes. I remember, in particular, a man who had gone through the worst of World War II. His memory was full of the horrors of battlefield carnage. But his heart was filled with the assurance that God doesn't fall off His throne when humans have problems, and that his salvation doesn't fly away when his emotions go out of control.

At the time I met the man he was suffering from serious depression. After a number of sessions together, when it seemed that I could be of no great help to him, he was able to say, "I don't want sympathy, just understanding. God is in this, too, and He will see me through it." His last bastion of defense was a sovereign God. He believed in Him in a way that ultimately commanded a yielding of emotions to Him.

Ownership of Self

The second theological characteristic of the poor coper is the suffering he goes through because he is owner of himself. As owner he has responsibility for how his life should come out. But he is finite in a bewildering and infinite creation, and so he is thoroughly lost.

It's a fact that we become emotionally possessive of the things we own. We are emotionally bothered when our property is damaged, lost, or stolen. I remember the day I lost a seven iron from my new set of golf clubs. I was shocked at how much that tool meant to me. I was emotionally involved. My daughter was depressed for two weeks when her cat took a walk and never returned. She was emotionally involved in the little yellow animal. So it is with the ownership of self. When we possess our own ego and it gets hurt, we are crushed. One Sunday evening I had feebly attempted to sing a solo in church. My son came to me afterward and said, "Not bad, Dad,

140

your voice only cracked twice!" I was humiliated.

How different for the one who believes fully that he is not his own, but is possessed by another—the living God. He has willingly turned over title of himself to God. Then there is no more to protect, so no loss need be suffered. One day you are going to turn it all over to God anyway, so why not do it willingly now?

Someone has said that we are born without our consent and will die against our will, but between those events we act as if we were our own by our own choosing. I believe it was Bishop James Pike who once said that being a Christian is dying once so he won't have to do it again.

twelve

How to Cope Well in Crisis

"Andy, what do you do when trouble really comes?"
Amos asked on an old radio show years ago.

"I just shut my eyes until it goes away," he drawled
in reply. Unfortunately a number of people have little
better method than that to help themselves through the
big events of life.

But we can do better than we do. Knowing how crisis
and change affect us and what techniques are appropriate and inappropriate will aid considerably. People who
cope well in crises have several recognizable characteristics: They honestly express grief and pain; they convert uncertainty to manageable sized risks and tasks;
they acknowledge increased dependency; they avoid
impulsive action; they avoid the "magic of the mouth";

they relieve tension constructively with work, play, diversion, exercise, entertainment; they recognize guilt for both winners and losers in any great change; they have had little "shame tax" imposed; they will discuss the problem—see anxiety as health, not illness; they stay close to people without clinging or withdrawing; they have achieved psychological integrity; they have previously coped well in crisis and change; they have good realistic information to work with; they are in good physical condition; they have cut short their own catharsis and grieving; they have genuine spiritual hope; they do not suffer from ownership of self.

Openly Express Feelings

In chapter 3, I mentioned the way Jesus wept openly at the tomb of Lazarus. If Jesus had had some normal Christian friends around they would have told Him not to cry. That is the usual counsel in our culture these days. Lazarus was about to spring out of his tomb anyway, so why all the fuss? Just calm down, and in a few minutes all will be resolved.

Real loss commands real feeling. People who cope well are free to express grief and pain openly and honestly. But the person who copes poorly may never shed a tear. He has become so repressed or suppressed that genuine emotion is stifled. Instead it boils away inside, giving him physical pain or a sour personality. Freely vented emotions are the healthiest. A person is better able to adjust if he honestly expresses his feelings rather than dishonestly inhibiting them.

But related to the honest expression of feeling is the ability to cut short one's own catharsis. The inept coper may be grieving openly, but getting him to cease is another story. The crisis victim may be converting the situation into a solicitation of sympathy leading to unhealthy dependency. Then he will be less prepared to cope than ever before.

A widow grieved for thirty years for her departed husband. She had been dependent all her life. She leaned upon her husband for a good share of the housework as well as decision-making in every turning point in their life together. Even as he lay ill and was certain of death he was making decisions she should have been assuming. When he died she was shattered.

And she stayed shattered for three decades. Had she had a normal grieving experience she would have returned to most of her normal emotions within a year and made definite steps for the use of her time in worthwhile activity, service, or employment. But she let self-pity be her lot. In most successful recoveries, the victim comes to the point of unconsciously choosing to be troubled no longer and to cease grieving.

Choose Manageable Tasks

The second trait of the person who successfully handles great changes in life is the capacity to convert uncertainty to manageable sized risks and tasks. People who have successfully come through political and social upheaval often discuss their experiences in terms of the smaller tasks which they were able to handle in the heat of the situation.

I listened intently as missionaries discussed their evacuation from an African country going through the birth pangs of political independence. Reliable information was so scarce that every decision was doubtful. Large, sweeping administrative decisions had to be made, but a host of important minor events had to be handled as well.

The first decision was to evacuate the women and children. This meant separations and worrying over those sent away and those left behind. It meant controlling anxiety for days at a time when no information could be obtained. In this chaotic milieu, the men organized themselves and assigned tasks. One group managed to keep water and food supplied. Another kept an eye on the jungle airstrips watching for planes. Another manned the ham radio. Still others were responsible for keeping up good relations with the native population that was perhaps more confused in the circumstances than anyone. But morale was high and good humor abounded. No one sat around. They converted their situation to manageable sized risks and tasks. No one tried to solve the whole independence question in a single morning.

Humor is an important element in crisis. During the evacuation, one of the men was preparing breakfast. He thought he was mixing up some powdered milk to drink. Instead it turned out to be pancake mix. He stirred it well, then tried to drink it. It was thick and mushy tasting. When he discovered his mistake, he shouted to his helpers, "Hey, guys, what do I do now?" "Sit on the stove and drink syrup!" came back the reply. Never fail to find humor and never deny humor in the midst of crisis. It will ease the pain and can become a genuine asset. It will quickly puncture any efforts to adopt a "poor me" attitude in the struggle.

A manageable sized task may be nothing more than keeping up a minimum of housework during the tempo of rapid change. It may mean making a list of people to call to be sure one's affairs are in order, or finding odd moments to pursue one's usual avenues of service. One symptom that a person is overwhelmed and not coping is in the noticeable reduction of personal care activities on the part of the victim. He may withdraw completely from the simpler maintenance tasks of living. If a person keeps these small items well managed it is a sign that he is handling the larger matter reasonably well.

An Acceptable Dependency Relationship

But we also need to recognize our increased dependency when we are in serious trouble. We may have to accept a friend's financial assistance even though it hurts our pride terribly. We may need to rely on people for favors we have no hope of being able to return. The successful coper works out a dependent relationship without excessive clinging and without sacrifice of personal integrity. When the crisis is over he is not plagued with the necessity of returning every single favor done for him. He will not feel beholden to every one who has extended a kindness. Instead he will view the situation as an opportunity to experience the economy of grace as perhaps never before. He will repeat the experience of receiving God's free gift of salvation in miniscule form. That is, he will be accepting significant gifts without regard to his status or capacity to earn them, and he will be unable to return them.

I know people who have never learned to accept a gift without returning in kind. Until the return has been made they are uncomfortable and apologetic. They bear a heavy "gift debt"—those awful feelings that somebody gave you something and you didn't get even by making a similar gift. But when God gave us life in His Son, He didn't insist on a return; the gift was truly free and everyone who accepts it can have it. The debt has been paid. If we can learn to accept God's great gift, we can also learn to accept smaller gifts from others without one compulsion to repay them.

Avoid Impulsive Action

The person who copes well has the capacity to avoid

impulsive action. This capacity is immensely important because most of the great changes in life involve large decisions financially, relationally, and in many other ways. Furthermore, tension runs high during the impact phase of crisis and it appears, to the victim, that some sweeping action would release the tension. And it may. But it may also set up a second problem greater than the first.

I worked with a man who had spent 17 years with a large public utility. Then a financial difficulty arose with the company and my friend lost his job. He was shattered. He had built his life around the company. When he was discharged he was offered the opportunity to receive his accumulated pension funds in one lump sum or to leave them with the company for investment for his retirement. Since the company had had a financial problem he didn't trust them to manage his money. He felt like indulging himself after his loss, so he could hardly wait to get his hands on 17 years of accumulated assets.

You can guess the outcome. He took his retirement funds, bought a fancy new luxury automobile, and traveled and loafed for more than a year. But then his assets were gone. He was back pounding the streets looking for work, disillusioned about life, and without a penny of financial security. We worked at the same place for about a year, but he was so despondent that his work suffered and he was dismissed. When I last saw him, he was living off his aged mother, looking halfheartedly for employment.

My friend had made an impulsive decision in the midst of crisis and set himself up for more troubles. I have witnessed the same thing happen again and again, particularly among new widows. They are faced with problems they do not know how to measure and then receive a fair-sized life insurance check. The need for tension reduction prompts impulsive actions. They buy a new house, or put the money into some speculative venture. Insurance people tell us that a widow's benefits are usually spent in short order.

Avoid impulsiveness at impact; that's the lesson here.

Avoid the "Magic of the Mouth"

In the previous chapter, we discussed the "magic of the mouth" symptom—excessive eating, drinking, smoking, gabbing and the like—of those who cope poorly in life's changes. I think it is apparent from that discussion that avoiding the magic of the mouth is important in successful coping. The healthy coper is usually one who has such impulses under good control. He knows that these symptoms create their own problems apart from the crisis that is being faced.

Recently I spoke with a widow who had struggled with a weight problem most of her life. When her husband died she was strongly tempted to eat continually as a source of tension reduction. But she recognized from her previous struggles with weight that this would be devastating to her physical well-being. Instead, she made a special commitment to God to be a good steward of her physical resources. During her adjustment she performed exceptionally well and actually lost weight. She had to buy a whole new wardrobe to accommodate her slim appearance: a reward for coping well.

Instead of resorting to the "magic of the mouth," and to impulsive action, the healthy coper relieves his tension constructively. With work, active play, wholesome entertainment, and exercise, both mind and body are fit for the changes under way. In short, an active rather than a passive approach is best. It is common for people to become reclusive and inactive during grief periods or when many things are changing. But slices of time need to be saved for regular and routine activities. Keeping up the tennis appointment, the jogging session, the regular restaurant treat will aid.

It is also possible to divide one's experience without becoming schizoid about it. Divide it into times when you pursue your normal activity, and times when you concentrate on problem-solving. This will not work out perfectly well—your mind will be heavily preoccupied occasionally and you'll double fault in tennis more often than you normally do. But planning your time to include normal recreation or diversion indicates an active mental approach to the situation as well as providing healthy activity.

Realistic About Guilt

In chapter 3 we discussed the matter of guilt at some length. We pointed out that in crisis and change situations a number of people are usually involved, in the vicinity of the main problem. It is common for them to experience guilt as a result of their involvement. Children of divorcing parents feel guilt for their parents' breakup. Friends of dying persons feel guilt because they are still alive and well. Persons close to accident victims feel guilt because they feel less worthy than the victim and wonder why the better person should suffer.

The person who copes well recognizes that guilt accompanies crisis and change. He knows that guilt comes to both winners and losers in competition for advancement on the job. The successful employee who is promoted over his peers feels guilty about his superior status. The boss who must fire an incompetent underling feels guilt for his actions, though he knows the organization is better off as a result of his decision.

The one who copes well in crisis knows how to deal

with his temptation to feel guilty if he is the victim. A great truth is told in this regard in the Old Testament book of Job. Job was beset by calamitous events: loss of family members through death, loss of most of his assets through various disasters. As a result, a number of friends came to Job to comfort him. But they insisted that Job recognize his guilt as genuine. They decided that Job must be guilty of something because of the calamities that had befallen him. But Job would not yield to the temptation. He declared himself righteous.

The one who makes adequate adjustments in crisis has learned not to interpret his spiritual condition from either his emotions or the events that come his way. Instead he identifies himself with the spiritual facts of life—that his righteousness is a gift that can be accepted without repayment. Any calamity that follows is not a refutation of his forgiven state. He can resist the temptation to feel guilt in either success or failure. Therefore guilt does not confuse the readjustment problems as the crisis wanes.

An acquaintance of mine lived in a small town close to our home. He was an elected public official in his village, serving the community without salary. During his term of service serious personnel problems arose among village employees. A squabble erupted concerning the man who managed the financial affairs of the village. By virtue of his office, my friend was required to investigate the matter and propose a solution. As he investigated, he found a number of concerns, but no one item that could be determined to be the critical matter. Instead there was the problem of the boss and favorite employees currying mutual favor; some poor accounting procedures; and a general "don't care" attitude toward the employees. The employees, as a result, were sharply divided about working for their boss.

During the squabble, my friend began receiving anonymous phone calls presenting information that tended to vilify the village supervisor. The callers offered undocumented "evidence" that would indict the man central to the problem. Then they usually strongly implied that my friend was equally responsible for the problem and should resign from office.

For a time my friend was tempted to investigate the claims presented in these phone calls. But he soon discovered that it was a useless task. He found himself trying to find evidence that would clear himself of the guilt implied by the callers.

As he discovered his own motive, he realized that those anonymous people were playing games with his emotions. One day he suddenly realized, "I'm not a guilty party in this village brawl; why am I protecting myself so much?" From then on he was able to think more clearly and effect an adequate solution. He had learned to resist the guilt that was being imposed and free himself from the "shame tax" payments being extracted.

Refuse to Pay the "Shame Tax"

More often than not, the healthy mind has learned to refuse payment of the shame tax. The shame tax is a device used by inadequate people to reduce the potency of those whom they see as a threat to them. If their peers can be shamed, and will accept the shame, they have evened the psychological balances between them; the inadequate people can feel safer. The device often reduces the marginally secure person to insecurity. Even more adequate people may be temporarily confused by someone's attempt to impose the shame tax on them. In a crisis situation the shame tax doubly confuses matters.

The shame tax is widely used in our society. It is systematically wielded in political campaigns, for example. A political organization that did not use it in its efforts to unseat a rival would be thought of as toothless. In labor-management negotiations, each side uses it to gain some bargaining advantage. In the press, guilt and shame are implied for those who are opposed editorially by the media. I think it unfortunate that we find it necessary to resort to such tactics. Even more unfortunate is the fact that it is also used in the church. I hope grace will abound and subdue this deplorable mechanism.

Talk About the Problem

The healthy mind in crisis will discover that it helps to talk about the problem. In talking one finds that anxiety is a symptom of health, not of illness. This is an important discovery because the discomforts of anxiety are quite disturbing. Troubled people often ask how they can stop the anxious feelings from arising so frequently. Sometimes people feel anxious even when they are removed from the stress situation. The fact that such stress follows them around is indeed disturbing.

My usual first response to such questions is to ask questions. "Suppose you felt no anxiety? Suppose you felt joyous feelings about the problem you are in? Would that be the proper response?" Then I attempt to indicate that the fact that anxiety feelings can arise spontaneously is a good sign. Anxiety is the symptom of excess pressure working itself out. Such feelings can be regarded as part of the healing process.

Unfortunately many of us have learned that anxious feelings are wrong. This is usually backed with a scriptural injunction that we are to "be anxious for nothing" (Phil. 4:6). Therefore if one feels anxious, he is somehow out of sorts spiritually.

The answer to this dilemma is an easy one. Just read the rest of the passage in which the injunction against anxiety occurs. It declares that we are to expose our anxieties by prayer and the conscious attempt to let the peace of God dwell in our lives. The point is that anxiety exposed, especially exposed to the touch of God, is anxiety on its way toward reduction. If a person denies or represses his anxiety because he thinks it is wrong, he only adds to his problem. He bottles up his anxiety so that it must go underground and convert itself into physical symptoms or troublesome traits of personality and life-style.

The person least able to get through crisis and change is the one who has learned total dictatorial control over his feelings. Such control will be involuntary if continued long enough. The person may control his feelings to the point that he is unaware of them. Then his personality will become rigid, uptight, inflexible. When a major crisis comes, he will be unable to adapt. So regard your involuntary emotions as helpful in two ways. They may stimulate you to get together with someone who will let you talk without imposing a shame tax; and they indicate a natural, emotional healing process going on in your mind.

Stay Close to People

During great change or crisis it is best to stay close to people rather than withdraw. Tumultuous times provoke the altruistic tendencies in people; they are easily available to use when we are troubled. The successful coper works out a comfortable position in relation to others—not too close, yet not withdrawn so as to be hidden from view. If he appears too close, he seems to be clinging and willing to become dependent in an unhealthy way. If he is too far away, he is unavailable to

154

the ministrations that could and should be coming his way. This optimum distance indicates that he is accepting basic responsibility for himself, but will receive the needed help that others can give.

Psychological Integrity Intact

Every life is a dynamic arrangement of psychological forces. Needs, wishes, fulfillments, threats, motivations, satisfactions and aptitudes make up this dynamic arrangement. As a person grows he works out a balance of these forces in his life, adopting a characteristic style of adjusting to the changing circumstances in his life. This unique arrangement of forces and the person's style of adjusting we call the psychological integrity of the person. This integrity is the unique individuality of any person. The balance of forces has been achieved over a number of years by successfully learning about life through experience and achieving satisfaction in most adjustment efforts. As a result, the psychological integrity of each person is something that is to be respected. It has been achieved with considerable cost and effort and is not therefore the playground for others to manipulate.

The person who comes through the great changes in life in satisfactory fashion is the person whose psychological integrity has been well respected. The person who copes poorly is one whose integrity has probably been insulted, attacked, manipulated or destroyed. It is therefore highly important to recognize that one should help very carefully if called to aid in crisis.

If we study the manner in which the Holy Spirit works in life we can understand the importance of respecting a person's psychological integrity. The Spirit does not charge into life like a bull on a rampage. He does not force His way or His will upon any person. Instead He

155

operates with the consent of the person involved, no matter how slow it may be in coming. The Bible describes the Spirit as one who woos the heart. The Spirit is given to gentle nudging, not crowbar levering. He moves only with the agreement of the one under His influence and does not interfer uninvited.

We, too, should be careful about how we enter the lives of people. The basic rule is to enter with consent; the consent having been won by the competence of the helper and his careful manner.

This points up a problem. It is at impact that a person needs help the most. Yet at impact he may be unable to clearly give or deny consent to be helped. Therefore it is doubly important that care be taken by anyone who must take over major responsibilities in the life of another. He may be doing so without the consent of the victim. If so, he must be prepared to gently obtain that consent or to back off.

If he moves in with the consent of the victim, he must recognize that he is there only for a short period of time. The victim is not required to yield most decision making for any extended period of time. Conflicts occasionally arise between helper and victim, and they usually stem from unclear knowledge about who is in charge of the victim's life when the impact is waning. In the great majority of cases, the victim's decision should stand. Only in the case of victims who are psychotic and out of touch with reality should other conclusions be carefully drawn under the guidance of professionally trained people.

Good Information

The person who copes well has been provided with good information. He has not had to guess about matters of fact that are readily available. He has been able to derive for himself or have furnished to him accurate data. This applies to matters of a simple nature as well as to complex aspects of problems. Just knowing simple information about hospitals, policies of financial institutions, basic elements of law, transportation schedules, or the whereabouts of important persons who might also be involved, can become highly important in crisis. Having needed phone numbers handy, knowing where the extra set of car keys is located, and knowing what public officials or bodies can be consulted can be vital to successful coping.

Good Physical Condition

In addition to good information, good physical condition is vital to coming through crisis. The crew of a military aircraft was shot down over ocean waters. They bounced in a raft for several days before being rescued. All survived but one. That one yielded to despondency about the war some weeks previous to this crisis and had nurtured himself mostly on liquor since. The crisis came and he perished. His body would not stand the abuse brought by deprivation of food and water.

Spiritual Factors

As we saw in chapter 11, the person who copes poorly with crisis and change lacks a workable theology that can see him through his problems. In addition he suffers from ownership of self, which means he must take total responsibility for his life. Working with finite resources, he comes up short in an infinite, bewildering universe.

Spiritually, the successful coper has a theology that gives him genuine hope and comfort as well as a clear perspective. He is not at the mercy of whims and conditions created by man because he trusts in God through Christ. He knows he does not own himself because he

157

has been "bought with a price" by the very Lord of the universe.

The successful coper takes Romans 8:35,37 as his motto and waves it high in the face of crisis, stress and change:

> "Who shall separate us from the love of Christ? Shall tribulation, or distress, or persecution, or famine, or nakedness, or peril, or sword? ... But in all these things we overwhelmingly conquer through Him who loved us."